M000249999

SELF-PRESERVATION

An Engaging Substance Abuse and DUI/DWI Life Skills Program/Workbook for Developing a More Self-Reliant, Self-Empowered, and Self-Regulating Lifestyle

"We all exist in a state of self-preservation, or doing what we think we need to do to survive. Sometimes, as life happens, our actions can become skewed and based on faulty beliefs. To correct this, we need to honestly self-assess our lives while spending enough time, with enough information. It's from this self-aware, newly educated position that we can then move forward making the best decisions for our lives. The keys to success are honesty and a basic desire to be healthier. You decide to be honest and I'll show you the rest."

BY:

MICHAEL E. ESSER, BHT

Copyright © 2018 Michael E. Esser

Copyright © 2018 Michael E. Esser

All rights reserved. No part of this publication may be reproduced, distributed, or transmitted in any form or by any means, including photocopying, recording, or other electronic or mechanical methods, without the prior written permission of the publisher, except in the case of brief quotations embodied in critical reviews and certain other noncommercial uses permitted by copyright law. This material has been assembled for educational purposes. For permission requests, write to the publisher, addressed "Attention: Permissions Coordinator," at the email address provided:

Michael.E.Esser@gmail.com

Ordering Information:

Quantity sales. Special discounts are available on quantity purchases by corporations, associations, and others. For details, contact the publisher at the email address above.

Printed in the United States of America

Copyright © 2018 Michael E. Esser All rights reserved.
No part of this publication may be reproduced, distributed, or transmitted in any form or by any means

FROM THE AUTHOR:

I just want to briefly tell you about my beautiful daughter Nina.

Growing up Nina was a handful. She seemed to have a chip on her shoulder early in life and never did anything she didn't want to do. I was 17 when she was born and became a single-father by the time she was two. She was raised by a boy who hadn't yet even learned to be a man.

I remember when she first went to daycare, she bit one of the sitters and got kicked out. In kindergarten, they needed an extra aid to sit with her because she was so easily upset that she became known for flipping her desk over.

When I was 24 I remarried, and Nina quickly went from excited to have a woman in the house to spewing the most hurtful things a 7-year-old could. Why? Because she didn't like change. By the time she was 13, she was drinking and smoking and by 16 insisted she needed to go to Texas to find her "real mother." (It's what she felt was missing her whole life.)

Unfortunately, soon after meeting her mom they began using meth together.

The weird part of all this is that when she was with me, she was a kind, sweet, loving and caring little girl who had a contagious smile and a silly laugh. I didn't see this wild side of her at first; she did an excellent job of hiding it from me. It wasn't until she was almost 19 when I started getting calls from county jail asking for money or a sobbing call in the middle of the night to just talk, and of course to request that I send her a few bucks. I asked her to get help.

She was later diagnosed with a substance use disorder and bi-polar schizophrenia.

She began treatment and medications and began to show signs of improvement. Over the years I'd brought her home a dozen times only to wake up the next morning to her having left in the night or she'd tell me she's going to a "meeting" only to get a call a few days later telling me she was in some other state.

By the time she was 21, she was starting to do a lot better and wanted to go to Las Vegas to live with a sober friend and start her life. I nervously gave her my blessing and off she went.

Copyright © 2018 Michael E. Esser All rights reserved.
No part of this publication may be reproduced, distributed, or transmitted in any form or by any means

She called regularly, began to work, had her own place to live, and was for the most part on her way towards something better. Not perfect, but better. And what is ironic is that with all the risky situations she had put herself into and all the bad decisions she made over and over, she survived.

On October 9th, 2013, she was a passenger in her friend's truck; sober and driving home from work early in the morning when they were forced off the road by a man who decided he was going to get drunk at a party and drive drunk, again. Their truck flipped into a palm tree, collapsing the roof, and killing them both instantly. He had just completed his DUI counseling in Nevada, nine days prior.

His decision means that she doesn't get to have kids or get married.

His decision means I don't get any more hugs or smiles.

The other thing his decision did was make sure Nina wouldn't be running off in the middle of the night anymore because her ashes sit on a shelf in my home, where I am able to give her a kiss anytime I want, while I'm dusting off her urn.

The point is, whatever your struggles, whatever your pains, start working to fix them today. We are not promised tomorrow.

Know that when your healthy you repair relationships, you don't do anything to jeopardize the future, and you don't do anything to rob anyone else of theirs.

It's for these reasons that this workbook was created. After years in the behavioral health field, working with court ordered substance abuse, DUI, and life skills clients, I never found any all-in-one program's that quickly fostered engagement, built character through regular self-reflection, provided all the required educational elements, and promoted holistic growth and lasting change. I like to describe it as having a "self-preservation" mindset.

It's too late to save Nina's life, but it's not too late to save yours.

This workbook and its potential benefits are dedicated to Jea1nina, her two sisters Alexis and Addison and her two brothers Theodore and Collin.

Copyright © 2018 Michael E. Esser All rights reserved.
No part of this publication may be reproduced, distributed, or transmitted in any form or by any means

TABLE OF CONTENTS

Copyright © 2018 Michael E. Esser All rights reserved.
No part of this publication may be reproduced, distributed, or transmitted in any form or by any means

Copyright © 2018 Michael E. Esser All rights reserved.
No part of this publication may be reproduced, distributed, or transmitted in any form or by any means

HOW TO USE THIS BOOK

THE MISSION OF THIS MATERIAL IS TO PROMOTE SELF-RELIANT, SELF-EMPOWERED, AND SELF-REGULATING INDIVIDUALS THROUGH EDUCATION AND OPEN DISCUSSION.

This workbook was engineered using both evidence and practice-based methodologies and meant to help those with substance abuse issues, as well as those who find themselves with a DUI/DWI or illegal drug charge.

This material covers the fundamental elements of substance abuse/use disorder recovery with special attention given to the life skills needed for actual growth and lasting personal change.

The goals of this program/workbook:

- To promote isolating the individual from the thing that brought them to this point, as well as any/all illegal activity.
- To help the individual to understand why they do what they do and why they no longer want those things to be something that's part of their life.
- To help the individual gain the knowledge and desire to repair damaged relationships and to reconnect with healthy supporters/activities.
- To help the individual make amends and promote a healthier, more prosocial interaction with their community.
- At the end of this program, see the individual complete a stronger, smarter, and healthier person/member of society.

These 18 sessions (Level II Education/Level I Treatment) are meant to build on one another towards developing the desired prosocial attitudes in a group setting. If this workbook is being completed on an individual basis, it's suggested that a third party, like a counselor, sponsor, or coach, review the individuals progress throughout and prior to completion.

Remember, the mission of this material is to help individuals develop a more self-reliant, self-empowered, and self-regulating lifestyle through a series of self-assessment, education, and open discussion elements.

Copyright © 2018 Michael E. Esser All rights reserved.
No part of this publication may be reproduced, distributed, or transmitted in any form or by any means

GROUP PROCESS

Ideally, the structure of these groups is meant to allow individuals the opportunity to come together in a group setting and self-assess their lives over the past week, their goals for the upcoming week, and then quantify their answers on a scale of 1 to 10 while self-reflecting on them. In addition to sharing their own testimony from the past week, everyone is also actively listening to the testimonies of their peers and reflecting on those experiences as well.

Individuals one by one, actively share the results of their self-assessment with the group, prepared to receive active feedback. Then, as others share, actively listen and prepare to offer orderly feedback when appropriate.

Once everyone has shared, the "thought exercise" or educational portion of the session takes place. In this part of the group process, the sessions "thought exercise" material is read, explained, completed, and discussed.

Upon completion, the group leader will discuss the interactive portion of the assignment further with the group, allowing each member to share their responses to the session's questions or topic.

Once everyone has reflected and shared on this portion, the final part of the group process is to assign the "homework" of exploring the sessions *thought exercise*. This is a reflection exercise based on the week's topic that the client is to spend the week reflecting on where there may be need for growth in their lives.

EXAMPLE GROUP PROCESS

- Sign into group
- Sit down and complete self-assessment worksheets
- Individually share self-assessments/get feedback
- (Depending on length of shares, take break or transition)
- Introduce and complete planned weekly "thought exercise" work
- Share findings of weekly "thought exercise" as group discussion
- Assign "thought exercise" or reflection homework
- Conclude group

Copyright © 2018 Michael E. Esser All rights reserved.
No part of this publication may be reproduced, distributed, or transmitted in any form or by any means

READ PRIOR TO FIRST SESSION: GETTING INTO A NEW MINDSET

You need to read this section BEFORE your first session.

This exercise will help to get you in the right mindset to make the changes or to reinforce the healthy, prosocial beliefs you are expected to maintain in society. It is designed to let you know just how hard you need to fight to ensure the circumstances that led you here aren't repeated. For some of us, having to comply with all the time, restraints, and costs the legal system may put on us is enough to change. For others it might take a little more effort.

This isn't necessarily going to be easy and you might have some unforeseen struggles moving forward. But know that when you're honest with yourself and have a desire to survive, to self-preserve, there's nothing that can cross your path that you won't stand up to.

It's with healthier boundaries and a "win-win" attitude that we now need to exist. It sounds extreme, but they say when it comes to addiction and criminal activity that there are only three possible long-term outcomes; recovery, jail, or death. We need to fight like its life or death, because it is.

These things that come against us might not have been meant for evil, but in our lives, they have become just that. They have been put on our "enemy list" because of the havoc they've helped foster in our lives. They are our fiercest opponents in the most dangerous places of our life and if we don't get truly angry when they come around and try to take us down, then they will continue to slip through the cracks until we don't have the strength we need to defeat them.

We need to get mad when that thief called "addiction" or "criminal activity" tries to infiltrate and take our lives away. We need to fight back with all we have when that "thing" threatens to kidnap us from our family and friends.

Our goal now is to begin to adopt new, or renewed, healthy behaviors while ending the old, unhealthy ones that have caused so much hurt. With your mind pointed in the right direction know that there is going to be more to this than just brute force and willpower, it's going to take us looking inward. Some things will take patience and finesse, while others will require you to physically get involved in breaking down some of those walls you may have so efficiently been building up for some time now.

Copyright © 2018 Michael E. Esser All rights reserved.
No part of this publication may be reproduced, distributed, or transmitted in any form or by any means

In addition, we also need to understand that there are a few more "basic" elements that we need to adapt that will help with our overall lasting success. This means, in addition to what we'll be learning and sharing, we also need to pay special attention to things like:

OUR SLEEP SCHEDULE, OUR DIET, AND OUR PHYSICAL MOVEMENT

We'll cover more about this as we go, but for now we just need to understand the basics and obviously if anyone has any health issues or concerns, consulting our physician prior to starting any nutrition or exercise routine is important and adjust from there to meet our needs is key. Also know that this is all *optional*, but also *strongly* being suggested to help both your mind and body to have the best possible chance for lasting change, happiness, and health. This means:

TRY TO START SLEEPING BETTER

Starting now, we need to be getting enough regular, quality sleep if we're going to be healthy. That means getting our 6 to 7.5 hours with the same bedtime each day. After all, in the mental health world, this is the easiest thing we can do to improve how we function, period.

TRY TO START EATING BETTER

From here on, we need to pay attention to what we put in our bodies. This means eating healthier, drinking more water, and eat less sugar/bread. Try pairing healthy proteins with good carbs for your 2-3 main meals a day and instead of chips or candy, try nuts and fruit. Your body will quickly begin to thank you.

TRY TO EXERCISE AT LEAST 10-30 MIN A DAY

We now need to try to add some sort of physical exercise to our daily routines. This means moving our bodies with purpose. Something as simple as stretching out first thing in the morning and then taking a 10-minute walk with three 20 second bursts of increased activity like running spread throughout. That's it.

SLEEP + EAT + EXERCISE + LEARN + LOVE/APPRECIATE = HAPPIER, BETTER YOU

Breathe in deep these challenges ahead and exhale something worth living for.

Copyright © 2018 Michael E. Esser All rights reserved.
No part of this publication may be reproduced, distributed, or transmitted in any form or by any means

PRE-TEST – TRUE OR FALSE

___ In the U.S., nearly one-third of all traffic deaths involve alcohol

___ Drivers with .08 BAC+ killed in a crash were 4.5x more likely to have prior DUI

___ On average only 1% of those that drink, and drive are arrested each year

___ BAC stands for blood alcohol concentration

___ At any level BAC, younger people are not at a greater risk than older people

___ Alternatives to driving drunk/high are calling cab, take bus, designated driver

___ Relapse happens in stages; emotional, mental, and physical

___ Automatic thinking can get us in trouble if we have unhealthy beliefs

___ Addiction can be the result of some sort of personal disconnection in one's life

___ You are not responsible for your behavior or making any needed changes

___ Reconnecting with ourselves, our purpose, and others helps addiction

___ Being completely honest with oneself is essential for recovery

___ The body can only process 1 drink per hour so only time will sober one up

___ Empathy is putting yourself in someone else's place to better understand them

___ Personal boundaries are just about having 3 feet of space around you

___ Cravings are thoughts we have, and urges are actions we take

___ Having a healthy support network like mentors and healthy peers is important

___ Isolating yourself from others is an unhealthy way of coping with grief

___ Anxiety is a result of your amygdala perceiving that you are in danger

___ It's not important to identify your personal strengths when bettering yourself

___ Getting enough sleep each night is crucial to your mental and physical health

___ In addition; diet, exercise, knowledge, and love are all pillars of healthy living

Copyright © 2018 Michael E. Esser All rights reserved.
No part of this publication may be reproduced, distributed, or transmitted in any form or by any means

LEVEL II EDUCATION - SESSIONS 1-8 + FINALS (16 HOURS)

WEEKLY SELF-ASSESSMENT 1 – When we do regular self-assessment, we "actively" begin to learn more about ourselves and our lives. These regular reflections on our lives lets us strengthen the positive aspects we like and adjust negative ones we don't. Our mission is to continuously be building our skillsets while we continue to build our character. (COMPLETE/SHARE FOLLOWING)

What's been your "BIGGEST STRUGGLE" over this past week?

On a scale of (1-to-10), rate this week's "struggle": (NOT BAD 1 - 2 - 3 - 4 - 5 - 6 - 7 - 8 - 9 - 10 WORST EVER)

What's the "BEST THING" you did or that happened to you this past week?

On a scale of (1-to-10), rate this week's "best thing": (OKAY 1 - 2 - 3 - 4 - 5 - 6 - 7 - 8 - 9 - 10 BEST EVER)

What's the "MOST IMPORTANT THING YOU SHOULD BE DOING" this upcoming week?

On a scale of (1-to-10), rate how important it is to do "this thing": (NOT 1 - 2 - 3 - 4 - 5 - 6 - 7 - 8 - 9 – 10 VERY)

What would you rate your motivation this week? (NONE 1 - 2 - 3 - 4 - 5 - 6 - 7 - 8 - 9 – 10 TONS)

What would you rate your week overall? (ROUGH 1 - 2 - 3 - 4 - 5 - 6 - 7 - 8 - 9 – 10 AWESOME)

Was this past week better than the week before?   (YES) - (NO) - (SAME)

Finally, for every question you rated less than a 10, go back and ask yourself, "What made it less than a 10?" Then ask yourself, "What would it take for me to rate that question an 8+?" (These answers identify something we need to work on and what we need to do to fix it.)

Copyright © 2018 Michael E. Esser All rights reserved.
No part of this publication may be reproduced, distributed, or transmitted in any form or by any means

THOUGHT EXERCISES - SESSION 1: SELF-PRESERVATION/BAC/PLEDGE

Self-preservation, noun: the protection of oneself from harm or death, especially regarded as a basic instinct in human beings and animals.

Self-preservation ensures we have a satisfying, and productive life. It helps us to maintain what we already have and to grow and develop in ways that allow us to meet challenges in the future. It helps us stay on track.

This means give an honest, healthy adult enough time and enough information and they'll make the best decision for their life. The key is to be *honest,* while becoming *healthier and* more *informed* over *time.*

This philosophy of honesty and growth is one that you need to become familiar with as we work through this program. You should want to survive and thrive. Maslow's hierarchy of needs describes the basic needs all humans have. They include the need for basic-necessities like food and water, the need for the security both in shelter and a community, the need for healthy relationships, the need for a good, healthy self-esteem, and finally a need to grow and explore ourselves for our own edification, or improvement.

It's in this honest growth that we then choose healthy prosocial options versus the dangerous and illegal antisocial choices that may have brought us here. Throughout this workbook you'll be given plenty of information and time to come to your own best conclusion as to what you want for your life. To get started, we need to cover an aspect of use that affects us all, DUI/DWI'S and drug charges.

<u>STATISTICS</u>

- In 2015, 10,265 people died in alcohol-impaired driving crashes, accounting for nearly one-third (29%) of all traffic-related deaths in the United States.

- In 2015, nearly 1.1 million drivers were arrested for driving under the influence of alcohol or narcotics. That's one percent of the 111 million self-reported episodes of alcohol-impaired driving among U.S. adults each year.

- Drugs other than alcohol (legal and illegal) are involved in about 16% of motor vehicle crashes.

Copyright © 2018 Michael E. Esser All rights reserved.
No part of this publication may be reproduced, distributed, or transmitted in any form or by any means

- Marijuana users were about 25% more likely to be involved in a crash than drivers with no evidence of marijuana use, however other factors – such as age and gender – may account for the increased crash risk among marijuana users.

WHO IS MOST AT RISK?

Young people:

- At all levels of blood alcohol concentration (BAC), the risk of being involved in a crash is greater for young people than for older people. Among drivers with BAC levels of 0.08% or higher involved in fatal crashes in 2015, nearly three in 10 were between 21 and 24 years of age (28%). The next two largest groups were ages 25 to 34 (27%) and 35 to 44 (23%).

Motorcyclists:

- Among motorcyclists killed in fatal crashes in 2015, 27% had BACs of 0.08% or greater. Motorcyclists ages 35-39 have the highest percentage of deaths with BACs of 0.08% or greater (37% in 2015).

Drivers with prior driving while impaired (DWI) convictions:

- Drivers with a BAC of 0.08% or higher involved in fatal crashes were 4.5 times more likely to have a prior conviction for DWI than were drivers with no alcohol in their system. (9% and 2%, respectively).

Source: https://www.cdc.gov/motorvehiclesafety/impaired_driving/impaired-drv_factsheet.html

ILLEGAL DRUG CHARGES

- In 2016 the U.S. population was estimated at 250,017,636 people, of which a total of 1,186,810 arrests for drug law violations were made, which means less than .05% of people were charged with a drug related crime. 84.7% possession and 15.3% sale or manufacturing of a drug.

Source: https://ucr.fbi.gov/

ALTERNATIVES TO DRIVING UNDER THE INFLUENCE

What are 3 alternates to drinking and driving or driving under the influence?

1. *CALL A CAB*   2._____   3. _____

Copyright © 2018 Michael E. Esser All rights reserved.

No part of this publication may be reproduced, distributed, or transmitted in any form or by any means

THOUGHTS/BELIEFS REGARDING SUBSTANCE USE, DUI'S, AND ILLEGAL DRUGS

Remember, this is your workbook. It's private and you are not being graded.

Do you feel you have a problem with drugs or alcohol?

How did you find yourself in this situation?

Think about the events or arrest that got you here. Is there any connection between day/night, weekday/weekend, summer/winter/season that jumps out as a particularly tough time for you emotionally, physically, financially?

Do you think illegal substance possession and/or DUI laws are fair?

Is it okay to buy, sell, or possess illegal drugs?

Is it okay to drive without insurance or a valid license?

What would you tell your child or close friend to try and stop them from finding themselves in a similar situation?

B.A.C. EFFECTS

- **.30 -. 50** Death may occur at .37 or higher. BACs of .45 and higher are fatal to nearly all.
- **.25 - .50** Very drunk. May lose consciousness.
- **.15** Obviously drunk. Staggering, weaving, irrational behavior.
- **.12 - .15** Vomiting may occur. May be drowsy. Loss of critical judgment, major impairment.

Copyright © 2018 Michael E. Esser All rights reserved.
No part of this publication may be reproduced, distributed, or transmitted in any form or by any means

- **.10** Loss of inhibition. Judgment and driving impaired. Clear deterioration of reaction time.
- **.08** Judgment and driving impaired. Defines intoxication in most states.
- **.06** Judgment and driving somewhat impaired.
- **.05** Definite relaxation. Most people are very mellow at this point. Some impairment.
- **.04** Most people begin to feel relaxed, sociable, and talkative.
- **.02** Moderate drinkers may feel some relaxation and warmth.

Calculating Your BAC

To estimate your own personal limit to avoid problems related to drinking and driving violations, the three things you need to know to calculate BAC:

1. Your weight.
2. How many drinks you have had.
3. The amount of time that you have been drinking.

Complete the following steps to determine your BAC.

Step 1. Body Weight: Fill in the blank with your weight. _____

Step 2. BAC Chart: Using the appropriate BAC Chart below (note male and female charts), find the row that is closest to your weight. If your weight is between two rows, use the lower weight row to make sure that you will be within legal limits.

MALES	NUMBER OF DRINKS									
WEIGHT	1	2	3	4	5	6	7	8	9	10
100	.043	.087	.130	.174	.217	.261	.304	.348	.391	.435
125	.034	.069	.103	.139	.173	.209	.242	.278	.312	.346
150	.029	.059	.087	.116	.145	.174	.203	.232	.261	.290
175	.025	.050	.075	.100	.125	.150	.175	.200	.225	.250
200	.022	.043	.065	.087	.108	.130	.152	.174	.195	.217
225	.019	.039	.058	.078	.097	.117	.136	.156	.175	.195
250	.017	.035	.052	.070	.087	.105	.122	.139	.156	.173

Copyright © 2018 Michael E. Esser All rights reserved.
No part of this publication may be reproduced, distributed, or transmitted in any form or by any means

FEMALES	NUMBER OF DRINKS									
WEIGHT	1	2	3	4	5	6	7	8	9	10
80	.053	.106	.156	.212	.265	.318	.371	.424	.477	.529
100	.050	.101	.152	.203	.253	.304	.355	.406	.456	.507
125	.040	.080	.120	.162	.202	.244	.282	.324	.364	.404
150	.034	.068	.101	.135	.169	.203	.237	.271	.304	.338
175	.029	.058	.087	.117	.146	.175	.204	.233	.262	.292
200	.026	.050	.076	.101	.126	.152	.177	.203	.227	.253
225	.022	.045	.068	.091	.113	.136	.159	.182	.204	.227

Step 3: Calculate your BAC Subtract your number in the table below from the number on the appropriate BAC Chart above to calculate your approximate BAC.

Time Factor Table								
Hours Since First Drink:	1	2	3	4	5	6	7	8
Subtract from BAC	.015	.030	.045	.060	.075	.090	.105	.120

[BAC Chart #] _____ - (minus) **[Time Factor Table #]** _____ = **[BAC]** _____

Step 4: Staying Safe There are two ways to ensure that your BAC level does not impair your ability to drive:

1. Pace your drinks so you never result in a total BAC level of .08 or greater.

2. Allow enough time after drinking for your body to eliminate enough alcohol.

If you drink enough alcohol to go beyond a BAC level of .08, you should not drive. Instead, find another person to drive you, or call a cab.

Source: *afterdeployment.org*

Copyright © 2018 Michael E. Esser All rights reserved.

No part of this publication may be reproduced, distributed, or transmitted in any form or by any means

PLEDGE TO YOURSELF, YOUR FAMILY, AND THE COMMUNITY

I pledge to not drink/use mind altering drugs - illegal or prescription - and drive; I will use a designated driver, call for a ride, find other transportation or make other arrangements prior to becoming impaired. I also pledge to speak up if I'm aware someone else is under the influence and preparing to drive.

I pledge to always make sure everyone in my vehicle buckles up and wears their seat belts, include myself.

I pledge to discuss traveling too fast for road conditions: sand storms, black ice, and fog as well as proper traveling distance between cars for road conditions whenever I am in the vehicle.

(Sign here): _____

IS THERE ANYTHING YOU'D LIKE TO ADD TO YOUR PLEDGE? IF SO, ADD IT HERE:

(Sign here): _____

Copyright © 2018 Michael E. Esser All rights reserved.
No part of this publication may be reproduced, distributed, or transmitted in any form or by any means

WEEKLY SELF-ASSESSMENT 2 – (COMPLETE/SHARE FOLLOWING)

Rate your SLEEP quality this week 1-10: _____ Rate your HEALTHY EATING this week 1-10: _____

Rate your EXERCISE/PHYSICAL ACTIVITY this week 1-10: _____

What's been your "BIGGEST STRUGGLE" over this past week?
On a scale of (1-to-10), rate this week's "struggle": (NOT BAD 1 - 2 - 3 - 4 - 5 - 6 - 7 - 8 - 9 - 10 WORST EVER)
What's the "BEST THING" you did or that happened to you this past week?
On a scale of (1-to-10), rate this week's "best thing": (OKAY 1 - 2 - 3 - 4 - 5 - 6 - 7 - 8 - 9 - 10 BEST EVER)
What's the "MOST IMPORTANT THING YOU SHOULD BE DOING" this upcoming week?
On a scale of (1-to-10), rate how important it is to do "this thing": (NOT 1 - 2 - 3 - 4 - 5 - 6 - 7 - 8 - 9 – 10 VERY)
What would you rate your motivation this week? (NONE 1 - 2 - 3 - 4 - 5 - 6 - 7 - 8 - 9 – 10 TONS)
What would you rate your week overall? (ROUGH 1 - 2 - 3 - 4 - 5 - 6 - 7 - 8 - 9 – 10 AWESOME)
Was this past week better than the week before?   (YES) - (NO) - (SAME)
Finally, for every question you rated less than a 10, go back and ask yourself, "What made it less than a 10?" Then ask yourself, "What would it take for me to rate that question an 8+?" (These answers identify something we need to work on and what we need to do to fix it.)

Copyright © 2018 Michael E. Esser All rights reserved.

No part of this publication may be reproduced, distributed, or transmitted in any form or by any means

THOUGHT EXERCISES -SESSION 2: CONTROLLED THINKING VS. AUTO THINKING

GOALS

- Discover how we've learned to "do what we do" from the different situations we've experienced in life and how we can challenge ourselves to be honest and to make better choices.

- We want to see where our automatic thinking has taken us and what controlled thinking can offer us moving forward.

DEFINITIONS

- <u>Automatic thinking</u>: Decision making that is based solely on past experiences and done without thinking the costs and benefits through.

- <u>Controlled thinking</u>: Decision making that considers past experiences, but also considers the pros and cons of our choice before acting. (Ex: Imagine time travelled to see how it might end, before we make any final decisions.)

THROUGHOUT LIFE, THIS IS HOW WE LEARN:

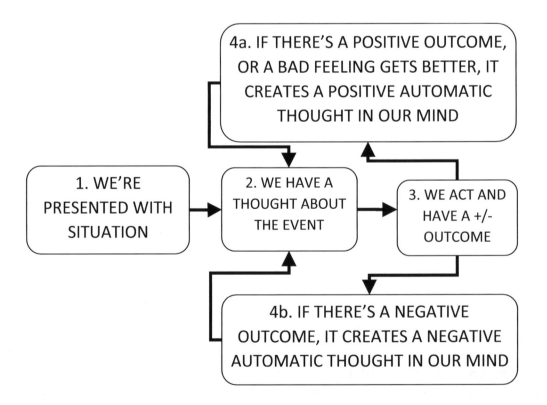

Copyright © 2018 Michael E. Esser All rights reserved.

No part of this publication may be reproduced, distributed, or transmitted in any form or by any means

THESE THOUGHTS >LEAD TO ACTION >WHICH LEAD TO FEELINGS:

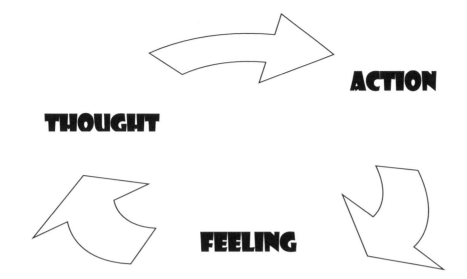

In our own stories, we have gone through our own ups and downs. We've all had things happen in our lives that made us feel good and want to do better and events that made us angry and feel like we couldn't trust anyone, or that we needed to act selfishly.

We all regularly learn from these positives and negatives in our lives and it's in all these continuous, layered choices that we form our beliefs. It's how we learn things and how we build our character. These choices get either strengthened or weakened based on how those choices work out for us.

EXAMPLE:

Let's say we went to a party as a teenager and had a few drinks or did some drugs and hooked up with someone we liked, we'd most likely wake up the next morning and think going to party's and drinking/using is awesome. That choice being positive would get strengthened in our automatic thinking process.

If that next weekend, we tried to recreate last weekend's results and figured a little booze and drugs were awesome, then a lot should be out of this world! Only now, in our stupor, we don't attract that special someone, make a fool of ourselves, and wake up the next day with a hangover. That choice being negative would get strengthened in our automatic thinking process.

Copyright © 2018 Michael E. Esser All rights reserved.
No part of this publication may be reproduced, distributed, or transmitted in any form or by any means

Living life from that point on we would add to our beliefs about substances when, after we broke up with someone we thought drowning our tears in liquor would help us forget or that celebrating our new promotion with a drug fueled bender was the "Hollywood" way to go. These choices, and the consequences stemming from them, all add to our automatic thinking process and then simply become second nature to us.

Now the next time we are presented with a similar situation or stressor, we will automatically resort to what has worked for us in the past. This is where we can run into problems because, as we respond to stress in life by always automatically choosing to drink or use and our bodies become more and more used to that being the solution to our problem and soon will begin to demand that solution for every little situation.

HOW TO STOP THE CYCLE OF AUTOMATIC THINKING

We need to train ourselves to slow down or STOP while we are working to gain better control of our thoughts.

- We need to practice being put into a variety of situations and imagining ourselves making the choice we typically would.

- We need to have that "mental time traveling" OR "playing of the tape" include all the vivid detail we can so that we can envision the worst-case scenario as the final outcome. After all, that is a possibility.

- We need to then think about making a different, better choice and having that scenario now play out in our mind with it leading to the best possible final outcome.

- Now, after running ourselves through both scenarios, we can move forward and make a decision based on our controlled thoughts and not just our automatic response.

We can do this with anything and everything in our lives. From our choices in high risk situations and environments like drinking and driving or breaking the law to healthy decisions about things like our nutrition and entertainment options.

Copyright © 2018 Michael E. Esser All rights reserved.
No part of this publication may be reproduced, distributed, or transmitted in any form or by any means

Some of us already have a pretty good grasp on this process and sometimes just need a simple refresher. While others need to simply be made aware of this process, so we can implement them into our own lives.

In time, like a muscle, this process will grow easier and you will grow stronger using it. Understanding how new events change and add to your character is crucial, and in time, this will all become part of your regular reasoning process.

RESPONSIBILITY AND GROWTH

Draw a picture of who's responsible for YOUR thoughts, beliefs and actions in the first box and include a few details about your life – family job, hobbies, etc. this is you CURRENT STATE. In the second box, draw you ideal or GOAL REALITY and make it as detailed as possible. This is now a before and after roadmap for your life – or where you are and where you want to be. Getting from here to there takes you 1. Seeing the possibility, 2. Believing the possibility, and then asking yourself, "What do I need to do to reach this goal reality?" so you can then, 3. Act on that answer. (Remember, doubt is a killer of dreams.) *SOURCE: 2015 TEDTALK*

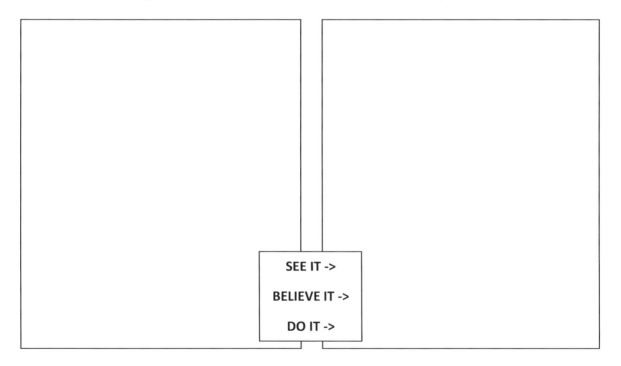

SEE IT ->

BELIEVE IT ->

DO IT ->

WHAT'S ONE WAY YOUR AUTOMATIC THOUGHTS HAVE CAUSED YOU PROBLEMS? (ANSWER AND SHARE)

Copyright © 2018 Michael E. Esser All rights reserved.
No part of this publication may be reproduced, distributed, or transmitted in any form or by any means

WEEKLY SELF-ASSESSMENT 3 – (COMPLETE/SHARE FOLLOWING)

Rate your SLEEP quality this week 1-10: _____   Rate your HEALTHY EATING this week 1-10: _____

Rate your EXERCISE/PHYSICAL ACTIVITY this week 1-10: _____

What's been your "BIGGEST STRUGGLE" over this past week?
On a scale of (1-to-10), rate this week's "struggle": (NOT BAD 1 - 2 - 3 - 4 - 5 - 6 - 7 - 8 - 9 - 10 WORST EVER)
What's the "BEST THING" you did or that happened to you this past week?
On a scale of (1-to-10), rate this week's "best thing": (NOT GREAT 1 - 2 - 3 - 4 - 5 - 6 - 7 - 8 - 9 - 10 BEST EVER)
What's the "MOST IMPORTANT THING YOU SHOULD BE DOING" this upcoming week?
On a scale of (1-to-10), rate how important it is to do "this thing": (NOT 1 - 2 - 3 - 4 - 5 - 6 - 7 - 8 - 9 – 10 VERY)
What would you rate your motivation this week? (NONE 1 - 2 - 3 - 4 - 5 - 6 - 7 - 8 - 9 – 10 TONS)
What would you rate your week overall? (ROUGH 1 - 2 - 3 - 4 - 5 - 6 - 7 - 8 - 9 – 10 AWESOME)
Was this past week better than the week before?   (YES) - (NO) - (SAME)
Finally, for every question you rated less than a 10, go back and ask yourself, "What made it less than a 10?" Then ask yourself, "What would it take for me to rate that question an 8+?" (These answers identify something we need to work on and what we need to do to fix it.)

Copyright © 2018 Michael E. Esser All rights reserved.
No part of this publication may be reproduced, distributed, or transmitted in any form or by any means

THOUGHT EXERCISES -SESSION 3: HOW ADDICTION WORKS

In our last session, we learned how we develop the thought patterns that have us believing and doing everything we do. Just to quickly recap, the idea is that we experience an event and that event has us thinking/feeling either positive or negative and we record that response, along with that event in our minds. It's layers and layers of this type of thinking that then creates our beliefs.

This is why when we find something that makes us feel positive or turns off negative feelings we tend to use that to fill the gaps, or disconnects, we perceive in our lives.

Most of the time, addiction starts when there's some sort of disconnect that's happening in our lives that our systems try to self-medicate because it is uncomfortable. For others, there may be a predisposition to how their systems react to the substances and a vicious cycle quickly takes hold. Either way, the idea that we've experienced or begin to experience some disconnect possibly because trauma, rejection, failure, low self-esteem, or some other perceived problem that we can't or don't immediately deal with in some sort of healthy manner has us seeking out or using a surrogate or alternative connection.

This connection will typically be with something that won't say "no" or reject us. It tends to be something we can control in a world we've deem out of control or uncontrollable. Even the idea that someone who simply likes to use because it's fun may be a sign of some sort of a social or self-soothing disconnect because the individual doesn't feel they can socialize or comfort themselves without the presence of the substance or surrogate activity.

It's from here that we then alter the way our brain works as the chemicals in our brain go from being used to a regular level of dopamine, to a tremendous flood of it. It is from this point that the brain can then become used to existing in a state of abundance and when it's given anything less, essentially throws a fit.

That's why quitting is so hard. This process becomes engrained in everything from our thoughts and beliefs to our actual cells. Take away those levels and change those activities and it's no wonder we get reports of life being boring when the honeymoon period of recovery ends. Because anything less than that elevated level of chemistry and the brain can't get excited anymore. It takes time and

Copyright © 2018 Michael E. Esser All rights reserved.
No part of this publication may be reproduced, distributed, or transmitted in any form or by any means

sobriety/abstinence from those substances for the brain to be comfortable working normally.

RECOVERY/RECONNECTING

First, we need to recognize the problem, do our homework about it, decide to want to change, and commit to being honest. (We'll discuss the stages of change in a few sessions.) We then need to understand that there has been a change to our brains and bodies and that disconnections in our world have taken place. We might immediately know what that is, or we might need to begin exploring ourselves for what that is/was. We do this with active sharing, active listening, and receiving feedback from others. (We'll get to this in the next session.)

We then need to continue those conversations and reconnections with healthy people, places, and things while eliminating or minimizing our contact with anyone, place, or thing we deem unhealthy for our recovery and reconnections.

Now we need to find, or rediscover, things we are passionate about along with things we find fun, like healthy hobbies or activities so we can begin to reward ourselves with them. We need to find purpose and any purpose at this point will do. We just need to be able to get out of bed and working towards that purpose so that we can reconnect with that part of ourselves. If that's a job, school, a project, or volunteering we need that foundational piece to the puzzle in place so we can build on it. (More on all of this later as well.)

All of this goes into our daily routine, along with; getting a good night's sleep, eating healthier, exercising a little each day, learning something new each day, and showing gratitude for what we have and those we have around us.

From that foundation we will start to build a better, healthier life. We'll start to discover things about ourselves we never knew and might even discover some hidden talents or skills that'll really change our world.

RECAP

- You need to do your homework and want to change the problem.

- You start talking about yourself and hearing what others have to say, you listen to others and offer them your honest feedback.

Copyright © 2018 Michael E. Esser All rights reserved.

No part of this publication may be reproduced, distributed, or transmitted in any form or by any means

- You surround yourself with supportive people, places and things, and eliminate any negatives or bad influences.

- You rediscover/discover your joy and passions, so you can reward yourself in healthy ways.

- Begin to focus on your purpose in life. (Family/work/school/volunteer)

- Look at how you sleep, eat, exercise, learn, and love/appreciate.

COST OF YOUR CHOICES/CHARGE

For many of us, the process of associating a COST to an event forces us to judge whether that event added value to our lives or if that event was unnecessary and a waste of our limited resources. If the event is deemed valuable, we typically will repeat it as desired. But, when an event is deemed unnecessary or wasteful, we typically will second guess going through it again or avoid it altogether.

LIST ANY COST YOU CAN RECALL REGARDING YOUR USE, OR CHARGES:

(EX. Alcohol/drug costs, court fees and fines, counseling fees, DMV/MVD fees, jail reimbursement, probation fees, car repairs, lost wages (hung over, time in jail, in group, at court, etc., lawyer, restitution, and any other misc. costs.)

_____
_____
_____
_____
_____
_____
_____
_____
_____
_____
_____
_____
_____
_____

TOTAL COST: _____ **(WAS IT WORTH IT?)**

Copyright © 2018 Michael E. Esser All rights reserved.
No part of this publication may be reproduced, distributed, or transmitted in any form or by any means

WEEKLY SELF-ASSESSMENT 4 – (COMPLETE/SHARE FOLLOWING)

Rate your SLEEP quality this week 1-10: _____ Rate your HEALTHY EATING this week 1-10: _____

Rate your EXERCISE/PHYSICAL ACTIVITY this week 1-10: _____

What's been your "BIGGEST STRUGGLE" over this past week?
On a scale of (1-to-10), rate this week's "struggle": (NOT BAD 1 - 2 - 3 - 4 - 5 - 6 - 7 - 8 - 9 - 10 WORST EVER)
What's the "BEST THING" you did or that happened to you this past week?
On a scale of (1-to-10), rate this week's "best thing": (NOT GREAT 1 - 2 - 3 - 4 - 5 - 6 - 7 - 8 - 9 - 10 BEST EVER)
What's the "MOST IMPORTANT THING YOU SHOULD BE DOING" this upcoming week?
On a scale of (1-to-10), rate how important it is to do "this thing": (NOT 1 - 2 - 3 - 4 - 5 - 6 - 7 - 8 - 9 – 10 VERY)
What would you rate your motivation this week? (NONE 1 - 2 - 3 - 4 - 5 - 6 - 7 - 8 - 9 – 10 TONS)
What would you rate your week overall? (ROUGH 1 - 2 - 3 - 4 - 5 - 6 - 7 - 8 - 9 – 10 AWESOME)
Was this past week better than the week before? (YES) - (NO) - (SAME)
Finally, for every question you rated less than a 10, go back and ask yourself, "What made it less than a 10?" Then ask yourself, "What would it take for me to rate that question an 8+?" (These answers identify something we need to work on and what we need to do to fix it.)

Copyright © 2018 Michael E. Esser All rights reserved.

No part of this publication may be reproduced, distributed, or transmitted in any form or by any means

THOUGHT EXERCISES -SESSION 4: ACTIVE SHARING-LISTENING-FEEDBACK

Self-preservation ensures we have a satisfying, and productive life. It helps us to maintain what we already have and to grow and develop in ways that allow us to meet future challenges. It helps keep us on track.

It sounds obvious, but it's important to understand that everyone on the planet is unique and we all experience life differently. We've begun to look at over the past few sessions the idea that at some point we all experience rejection, fear, trauma, etc. in life and that it might see us suffer some sort of "disconnect" from the world around us. We've learned that it's because of these "disconnects" that we as human beings tend to seek out alternative "connections" and that typically means we seek things that won't "reject" us and this could very well be things like; drugs/alcohol but also; food, gambling, sex, shopping, thrill seeking, etc. It's in these new surrogate "connections" being made in our brains that we find new comforts and a control of the process that is initially satisfying, but can lead us to develop addictions. We learned that for others there can be a predisposition to addiction and the introduction of a substance can trigger the addictive cycle.

The key to correcting this seems to be time, honesty, and in finding a way of reconnecting with ourselves and others. We do this last part by reevaluating our varied life experiences using active sharing and active listening techniques.

The basic idea is that we self-reflect on a topic and then share those personal thoughts with others with the understanding that we are ready to openly receive feedback from them. It is in this process that we can refocus and redefine our thoughts/beliefs based on this additional information and our new goals for life. (This is, in part, why we are doing regular weekly self-assessments.)

First, to illustrate this best we'll look at something called the "Johari Window" which is a tool that helps you better understand yourself and others. It was created in 1955 by psychologists Joseph Luft and Harrington Ingham, (Joe + Harry = Jo-Hari) and is used as a self-discovery exercise.

JOHARI WINDOW

Basically, what the Johari Window represents is you and what is known or unknown about you and your personality, tendencies, talents, etc. The window is divided into four areas. (See image on next page.)

Copyright © 2018 Michael E. Esser All rights reserved.

No part of this publication may be reproduced, distributed, or transmitted in any form or by any means

The upper left corner labeled "1. Open/free area" is the area of you that is public knowledge. It's what we all know about you, – you know these things, we know these things about you – it's the obvious stuff.

To the right of that box in the upper right side labeled "2. Blind area" we find the area of your life that you are blind or unaware of. It is things we all know about you, but you don't know about yourself.

Below in the lower left corner labeled "3. Hidden area" we find the area of your life that is known only to you. No one else in the world knows these secrets and thoughts about you.

Finally, on the lower right side of the window labeled "4. Unknown area" we find the area representing all the things about you that no one – including yourself – knows about you. It is in this area that shared, and self-discovery occur. It is in this area that you can find all sorts of unknowns like revelations and talents.

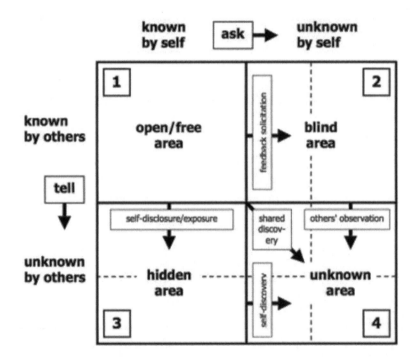

The healthier we are the larger our "open/free area" is and the more transparent we are. The mission from here on out is to grow this area of ourselves and we do this in a few ways.

Basically, we start by actively sharing something about ourselves or something we'd like to know to someone we trust – and that lets us tap into our hidden area because we are self-disclosing/exposing something previously unknown by others. We then actively listen to the trusted individual who then, after they've heard what we shared and are aware that we are looking for feedback, provides us with their insights and understandings on the topic – which lets us tap into our blind area because until now we were unaware of this insight.

Copyright © 2018 Michael E. Esser All rights reserved.
No part of this publication may be reproduced, distributed, or transmitted in any form or by any means

It is in this back and forth process of sharing and asking and receiving feedback that we experience growth of our open/free areas. We see the lines move as our hidden and blind areas shrink, open/free area grows, and we begin to tap into our unknown area which prompts shared and self-discovery.

Note that you don't have to agree with the feedback, and sometimes the truth hurts, but if you trusted the person enough to share, trust that they are hopefully responding honestly and with your best interests at heart. Physically or verbally rejecting feedback might shut down or filter the responses you are getting and that will most definitely hinder your growth. Take feedback as constructive and don't be afraid to share with multiple people so that you can get a consensus.

This process works both ways and so when someone actively shares with us, we have a responsibility to actively listen and give them our honest, respectful feedback. This process is called having a real "conversation" in an age when emoji's, text messages, emails, and posts do most of our communicating. It's a fundamental element to us reconnecting and bonding with our new, healthier world.

You're opening up and asking questions and sharing your private thought is the definition of active sharing. For active listening the idea is that we actually pay attention to the person talking to us, we give physical cues that we are listening by facing them, having appropriate eye contact, and giving the occasional nod. It means summing up what they are saying or parroting back the highlights of what they've shared when the conversation calls for it.

RECAP

- Be willing to share your thoughts and feelings honestly
- Ask questions
- Openly receive feedback
- Actively listen when others share
- Give honest, respectful feedback
- Self-reflect on your growth

Now that we're getting this ball rolling, let's put another import piece of the puzzle in place, a relapse prevention plan. This is a premediated, pre-thought out plan covering what we're doing/will do if we feel relapse starting to take place.

Copyright © 2018 Michael E. Esser All rights reserved.
No part of this publication may be reproduced, distributed, or transmitted in any form or by any means

BUILDING YOUR RELAPSE PREVENTION PLAN

Will you include any of the following in your relapse prevention plan?
Self-Help Programs like A.A., N.A., Celebrate Recovery, etc. *Yes or No*
A Proper Diet *Yes or No*
An Exercise Program Important *Yes or No*
A Spiritual Development Program *Yes or No*
Morning and Evening Inventories *Yes or No*

As a way of premeditating your response in the future, answer the following:
What direct action can I take when I am feeling lonely?

What direct action can I take when I am feeling nervous?

What direct action can I take when I am feeling frustrated or angry?

What direct action can I take when I'm not getting along with friends and family?

What direct action can I take when recovery begins to feel boring/unimportant?

Make a list of high risk people and places you will avoid:
High risk people I will avoid:
High risk places I will avoid:

Who is someone who can give you support in times of need? (Name/Number)

What are the signs and symptoms that indicate I am heading toward relapse?

What are the consequences if I relapse?
To Self:
To Family:
To Society:

What are the benefits if I remain in recovery?
To Self:
To Family:
To Society:

Copyright © 2018 Michael E. Esser All rights reserved.
No part of this publication may be reproduced, distributed, or transmitted in any form or by any means

WEEKLY SELF-ASSESSMENT 5 – (COMPLETE/SHARE FOLLOWING)

Rate your SLEEP quality this week 1-10: _____ Rate your HEALTHY EATING this week 1-10: _____

Rate your EXERCISE/PHYSICAL ACTIVITY this week 1-10: _____

What's been your "BIGGEST STRUGGLE" over this past week?
On a scale of (1-to-10), rate this week's "struggle": (NOT BAD 1 - 2 - 3 - 4 - 5 - 6 - 7 - 8 - 9 - 10 WORST EVER)
What's the "BEST THING" you did or that happened to you this past week?
On a scale of (1-to-10), rate this week's "best thing": (NOT GREAT 1 - 2 - 3 - 4 - 5 - 6 - 7 - 8 - 9 - 10 BEST EVER)
What's the "MOST IMPORTANT THING YOU SHOULD BE DOING" this upcoming week?
On a scale of (1-to-10), rate how important it is to do "this thing": (NOT 1 - 2 - 3 - 4 - 5 - 6 - 7 - 8 - 9 – 10 VERY)
What would you rate your motivation this week? (NONE 1 - 2 - 3 - 4 - 5 - 6 - 7 - 8 - 9 – 10 TONS)
What would you rate your week overall? (ROUGH 1 - 2 - 3 - 4 - 5 - 6 - 7 - 8 - 9 – 10 AWESOME)
Was this past week better than the week before?   (YES) - (NO) - (SAME)
Finally, for every question you rated less than a 10, go back and ask yourself, "What made it less than a 10?" Then ask yourself, "What would it take for me to rate that question an 8+?" (These answers identify something we need to work on and what we need to do to fix it.)

Copyright © 2018 Michael E. Esser All rights reserved.
No part of this publication may be reproduced, distributed, or transmitted in any form or by any means

THOUGHT EXERCISES - SESSION 5: SUBSTANCES AND THE BODY

Our reaction to the substances that are introduced into our bodies, and the psychological reasons behind our use, is something that may have become a problem. The idea that we might have once been able to go out and have fun at a party changed, and we no longer need the excuse of a party to alter our minds.

This session isn't meant to preach to you in any way and is instead going to serve the purpose of simply educating the individual about the main substances we find on the street and those drugs we see trending in our population.

CHEMISTRY OF ADDICTION

According to the National Institute of Drug Addiction:

- The brain is made up of many parts that all work together as a team.

- Drugs can alter important brain areas that are necessary for life-sustaining functions and can drive the compulsive drug abuse that marks addiction.

- The brain is a communications center consisting of billions of neurons, or nerve cells.

- Networks of neurons pass messages back and forth among different structures within the brain, the spinal cord, and nerves in the rest of the body (the peripheral nervous system).

- These nerve networks coordinate and regulate everything we feel, think, and do.

- Drugs are chemicals that affect the brain by tapping into its communication system and interfering with the way neurons normally send, receive, and process information.

- Some drugs, such as marijuana and heroin, can activate neurons because their chemical structure mimics that of a natural neurotransmitter.

- This similarity in structure "fools" receptors and allows the drugs to attach onto and activate the neurons.

Copyright © 2018 Michael E. Esser All rights reserved.
No part of this publication may be reproduced, distributed, or transmitted in any form or by any means

- Although these drugs mimic the brain's own chemicals, they don't activate neurons in the same way as a natural neurotransmitter, and they lead to abnormal messages being transmitted through the network.

- Other drugs, such as amphetamine or cocaine, can cause the neurons to release abnormally large amounts of natural neurotransmitters or prevent the normal recycling of these brain chemicals.

- This disruption produces a greatly amplified message, ultimately disrupting communication channels.

- Most drugs of abuse directly or indirectly target the brain's reward system by flooding the circuit with dopamine.

- Dopamine is a neurotransmitter present in regions of the brain that regulate movement, emotion, motivation, and feelings of pleasure.

- When activated at normal levels, this system rewards our natural behaviors. Overstimulating the system with drugs, however, produces euphoric effects, which strongly reinforce the behavior of drug use—teaching the user to repeat it.

- Our brains are wired to ensure that we will repeat life-sustaining activities by associating those activities with pleasure or reward.

- Whenever this reward circuit is activated, the brain notes that something important is happening that needs to be remembered, and teaches us to do it again and again without thinking about it.

- Because drugs of abuse stimulate the same circuit, we learn to abuse drugs in the same way.

- When some drugs of abuse are taken, they can release 2 to 10 times the amount of dopamine that natural rewards such as eating, and sex do.

Source: https://www.drugabuse.gov/publications/drugs-brains-behavior-science-addiction/drugs-brain

TYPICAL SUBSTANCES/DRUGS FACTS

Drugs are broken down into five classifications:

Copyright © 2018 Michael E. Esser All rights reserved.
No part of this publication may be reproduced, distributed, or transmitted in any form or by any means

- Sedatives/depressants/system suppressors that slow us down. Ex. Alcohol/sleeping pills/inhalants

- Narcotics/opiates/system suppressors that reduce pain/increase pleasure. Ex. Heroin/codeine

- Stimulants/speed/system enhancers that excite the nervous system. Ex. Amphetamines/ecstasy/cocaine

- Hallucinogens/mental enhancers that change perception of reality. Ex. mushrooms

- Cannabis/system suppressor AND enhancer that starts out stimulating the body before a feeling of relaxation sets in.

Each drug has its own unique DIRECT EFFECT, or what physically/psychologically happens while we are using the drug, and its own unique INDIRECT EFFECT, or what happens when we stop using the drug and it begins to wear off aka withdrawal.

DIRECT EFFECTS:

- Sedatives: drowsiness, slurred speech, depression, blackouts, impaired motor skills, poor judgement

- Narcotics: blocks pain, euphoria, relaxation, confusion, depression, poor judgement

- Stimulants: insomnia, euphoria, restlessness, talkative, weight loss, tremors, paranoia, panic, aggression, dehydration, impaired motor skills, poor judgement

- Hallucinogens: hallucinations, insomnia, euphoria, flashbacks, increased blood pressure, delusions

- Cannabis: stimulation, relaxation, impaired short-term memory/motor skills/reaction time, paranoia, drowsiness

INDIRECT EFFECTS:

- Sedatives: agitation, irritability, anxiety, fear, shakes, hallucinations, vomiting, insomnia, physical impairment

Copyright © 2018 Michael E. Esser All rights reserved.
No part of this publication may be reproduced, distributed, or transmitted in any form or by any means

- Narcotics: irritability, anxiety, fear, shakes, chills, sweating, nausea/cramping, physical impairment

- Stimulants: paranoia, headaches, fatigue, apathy, guilt, cravings, oversleeping, slowed motor skills

- Hallucinogens: depression, anxiety, paranoia, brain damage, delirium, loss of appetite

- Cannabis: anxiety, restlessness, impaired concentration, irritability, stomach aches, hostility

ALCOHOL FACTS

Different types of drinks have different alcohol concentrations, but a 1.25oz shot/mixed drink, a 5oz glass of wine, and a 12oz beer all have about .5oz of pure alcohol in them.

In most states, a blood alcohol concentration, or BAC, of .08 is considered impaired enough to be charged with a DUI and a BAC of .15+ is considered and extreme DUI. Figuring your BAC takes into consideration your gender, weight, number of drinks you had, how long it took you to drink them, and how long it's been since you drank.

When we drink, the alcohol enters the blood stream mostly via our small intestine. 98% of this alcohol is used up at a rate of one drink per hour on average. The other 2% exits through urination and breathing.

Risks from consuming alcohol on a regular basis/to excess are:

- Damages to the liver: fatty liver disease, cirrhosis

- Damages to the throat/digestive system

- Damages to the heart muscles/brain/nerves

- Damage to other organs like kidneys/pancreas/lungs

- Myopathy of the muscles/weakening of the muscles

- Immune systems are weakened

- Sexual reproduction/function for both sexes can be impaired/damaged

Copyright © 2018 Michael E. Esser All rights reserved.
No part of this publication may be reproduced, distributed, or transmitted in any form or by any means

- Withdrawals from alcohol can be deadly and medical detoxification is suggested for chronic users.

WHAT KIND OF DRINKER ARE YOU?

First, we want to determine what kind of drinker/drug user you are. This is important because it might be the first time you put a label on your use. Also, when we identify our patterns, we can use that information/ understanding to know where we stand and begin to make the types of changes we may need.

How much do you drink?

- o Mild – less than one drink a day
- o Moderate – one to two in a day
- o Severe – three or more in a day

How often do you drink?

- o Rare – once a month or less
- o Regularly – 1-3 days a week
- o Daily – 6-7 times a week

WHAT IS YOUR ALCOHOL PATTERN OF USE? _____

WHAT KIND OF DRUG USER ARE YOU?

How many types of drugs have you used?

- o None – never used anything – skip ahead
- o Single-drug – only used one drug
- o Multi-drug – have used more than one drug

How often do you use drugs?

- o Infrequent – once a month or less
- o Regularly – 1-3 days a week
- o Daily – 6-7 times a week

WHAT IS YOUR DRUG PATTERN OF USE? _____

Copyright © 2018 Michael E. Esser All rights reserved.
No part of this publication may be reproduced, distributed, or transmitted in any form or by any means

SOCIAL, INDEPENDENT, OR COMBINATION DRINKER/DRUG USER

Next, we want to determine our style of use and whether we are a social, independent, or combination drinker/drug user. We want to go through this process and determine our patterns and styles it's because it's in that knowledge that we can then begin to understand ourselves enough to start thinking about what it is that we want to do next.

Answer the following true or false questions:

T or F: Most of my friend's drink/use drugs

T or F: My social life mostly requires drinking/drug use

T or F: I mostly drink at bars with friends

T or F: I mostly use drugs with friends

T or F: I don't normally drink/use by myself

- If you've answered TRUE to more of these questions, you might be more of a SOCIAL drinker/user.

- If you've answered FALSE to more of these questions, you might be more of an INDEPENDENT drinker/user.

- If while answering these questions, you felt that you could waiver either way, you might be BOTH a SOCIAL and INDEPENDENT drinker/user.

Circle your use type: SOCIAL - INDEPENDENT - BOTH

BENEFIT FROM YOUR DRINKING AND DRUG USE

Finally, we want to determine the level of benefit that you get from your drinking and drug use.

Ask yourself the following:

I typically drink alcohol/use drugs (Mark ones that fit you):

- o To make myself happy/feel good

- o To lessen stress/depression

- o Fun with others

Copyright © 2018 Michael E. Esser All rights reserved.
No part of this publication may be reproduced, distributed, or transmitted in any form or by any means

- o Relax/calm down

- o To forget problems

- o Enhance my alertness/performance

- o Get along with people

_____ Total marked

Based on how many statements above that you related to/fit you we begin to get an idea of the benefits you get from your drinking/use.

CIRCLE ONE 1-2 = minimal benefit, 3-6 = significant benefit, 7-8 = extreme benefit

PUTTING IT ALL TOGETHER

WHAT IS YOUR ALCOHOL PATTERN OF USE?

Ex: Moderate/Regular drinker

(Write it here): _____ / _____ / DRINKER

Ask yourself, "Am I a predictable drinker?"

WHAT IS YOUR DRUG PATTERN OF USE?

Ex: Single/Daily drug user

(Write it here): _____ / _____ / DRUG USER

Ask yourself, "Am I a predictable drug user?"

(**Circle**) whether you're a *SOCIAL, INDEPENDENT, OR COMBINATION* drinker/user

Identify the benefit you get from your drinking and drug use (**Circle**):

MINIMAL BENEFIT - SIGNIFICANT BENEFIT - EXTREME BENEFIT

WHAT DOES IT ALL MEAN AND HOW CAN KNOWING ALL THIS HELP?

For starters, identifying our patterns lets us have better control of our schedule. Basically, we identify a behavior/activity we want to change and by knowing our own patterns we can begin to plan to change our schedules around to not allow us the time or opportunity to fail.

Copyright © 2018 Michael E. Esser All rights reserved.
No part of this publication may be reproduced, distributed, or transmitted in any form or by any means

By identifying whether we are a social or solo drinker/user, we can then begin to adjust for that as well. If we're a solo drinker/user and know we'll drink after work each night, we can plan to go to the gym, to a meeting, or change our schedule around so that we aren't alone during those times. If we're social drinker/user, then we can change who we hang out with, the events we do when we'd normally be drinking, or plan some alone time.

The benefits we get from our drinking/use let us know what we're trying to overcompensate for. Are we burying our feelings, past trauma, low self-esteem, antisocial behavior, social anxiety, bad relationships, etc.? Whatever it is, when we see what we are truly trying to connect with through our use, we can then put a plan in place to begin to repair or replace those connections/needs with healthier, sustainable options.

SHARE YOUR USE PATTERNS AND BENEFITS WITH YOUR GROUP/MENTOR. DID YOU ALREADY KNOW THESE ELEMENTS OF YOU LIFE OR WAS THIS SOMETHING NEW TO YOU? SHARE.

Copyright © 2018 Michael E. Esser All rights reserved.
No part of this publication may be reproduced, distributed, or transmitted in any form or by any means

WEEKLY SELF-ASSESSMENT 6 – (COMPLETE/SHARE FOLLOWING)

Rate your SLEEP quality this week 1-10: _____ Rate your HEALTHY EATING this week 1-10: _____

Rate your EXERCISE/PHYSICAL ACTIVITY this week 1-10: _____

What's been your "BIGGEST STRUGGLE" over this past week?
On a scale of (1-to-10), rate this week's "struggle": (NOT BAD 1 - 2 - 3 - 4 - 5 - 6 - 7 - 8 - 9 - 10 WORST EVER)
What's the "BEST THING" you did or that happened to you this past week?
On a scale of (1-to-10), rate this week's "best thing": (NOT GREAT 1 - 2 - 3 - 4 - 5 - 6 - 7 - 8 - 9 - 10 BEST EVER)
What's the "MOST IMPORTANT THING YOU SHOULD BE DOING" this upcoming week?
On a scale of (1-to-10), rate how important it is to do "this thing": (NOT 1 - 2 - 3 - 4 - 5 - 6 - 7 - 8 - 9 – 10 VERY)
What would you rate your motivation this week? (NONE 1 - 2 - 3 - 4 - 5 - 6 - 7 - 8 - 9 – 10 TONS)
What would you rate your week overall? (ROUGH 1 - 2 - 3 - 4 - 5 - 6 - 7 - 8 - 9 – 10 AWESOME)
Was this past week better than the week before?   (YES) - (NO) - (SAME)
Finally, for every question you rated less than a 10, go back and ask yourself, "What made it less than a 10?" Then ask yourself, "What would it take for me to rate that question an 8+?" (These answers identify something we need to work on and what we need to do to fix it.)

Copyright © 2018 Michael E. Esser All rights reserved.
No part of this publication may be reproduced, distributed, or transmitted in any form or by any means

THOUGHT EXERCISES - SESSION 6: PROSOCIAL V. ANTISOCIAL BEHAVIORS

Who would you become in a crisis like a car accident?

Using a crisis as a metaphor for those obstacles in our lives that we fear, but still must overcome, we build on our outward sympathy/empathy and inward prosocial/antisocial understandings and apply it to our lives.

SYMPATHY is an emotional response to something outside of ourselves and described as taking place AFTER the fact – AFTER you see someone's hurt or pain. ("Oh dang, they got hurt.")

RE-WRITE YOUR DEFINITION OF SYMPATHY AND DISCUSS:

EMPATHY is putting yourself in someone else's place, helps us to better understand that persons thoughts, feelings, and beliefs. Empathy happens BEFORE the pain. ("Oh no! They're going to get hurt!")

RE-WRITE YOUR DEFINITION OF EMPATHY AND DISCUSS:

WE CAN STRENGTHEN OUR ABILITY TO EMPATHIZE WITH SOMEONE BY:

SKILL 1: Centering on the person. (Look at them/listen to them/understand them.)

SKILL 2: Think and imagine being in the person's place.

SKILL 3: Accept the individual for what they are without judgement or blame.

SKILL 4: Reflect or state the other person's position to yourself and/or the other person.

SKILL 5: Listen back to your own and the other person's response.

Continuing with the crisis metaphor for those obstacles in our lives that we fear, but still must overcome, we build on our understanding with a look at antisocial, prosocial, and moral character.

ANTISOCIAL: To disregard and violate the rights of others or to do harm to others, or to go against the rules or laws of a society. (Illegal/criminal activity)

Copyright © 2018 Michael E. Esser All rights reserved.
No part of this publication may be reproduced, distributed, or transmitted in any form or by any means

RE-WRITE YOUR DEFINITION OF ANTISOCIAL:

PROSOCIAL: To respect the rights of others, to comply with what's thought of as normal, to abide by the rules/laws of society, and to live in harmony with the community we live in. (Our heroes.)

RE-WRITE YOUR DEFINITION OF PROSOCIAL:

MORAL CHARACTER: The moral/ethical views of a person or the feelings and thoughts we have about what's right and wrong and our ability to stick to our beliefs. (This will be what keeps you human.)

RE-WRITE YOUR DEFINITION OF MORAL CHARACTER:

FORTIFY YOUR MORAL CHARACTER/PROSOCIAL:

1. DEVELOP EMPATHY

2. KNOW YOUR PART IN SOCIETY

3. THINK ABOUT HOW YOUR ACTIONS AFFECT OTHERS

4. KNOW THAT YOU ARE A ROLE MODEL

5. THINK OF YOURSELF AS IMPORTANT

6. BE PART OF THE SOLUTION, NOT THE PROBLEM!

EXPLORING HOW THESE EVENTS ARE AFFECTING US

Having the desire to take charge and change our perceptions is a powerful process. To do this we must continue to build the discrepancy between what we think and what we do. We need to let this inconsistence bring clarity to what we are doing so that it can change the choices we make moving forward.

For this exercise, think about your life and how it has been affected by this/these events, how they will be if you don't change, and then what it'll be like if you do change.

Copyright © 2018 Michael E. Esser All rights reserved.
No part of this publication may be reproduced, distributed, or transmitted in any form or by any means

How has this affected my relationships with family and my loved ones?

If I continue using/committing criminal acts?

If I quit or stop?

How has this affected my relationships with friends?

If I continue using/committing criminal acts?

If I quit or stop?

How has this affected my career and educational path?

If I continue using/committing criminal acts?

If I quit or stop?

How has this affected my finances?

If I continue using/committing criminal acts?

If I quit or stop?

How has this affected my health?

If I continue using/committing criminal acts?

If I quit or stop?

How has this affected my long-term goals?

If I continue using/committing criminal acts?

If I quit or stop?

SHARE YOUR RESPONSES

Copyright © 2018 Michael E. Esser All rights reserved.
No part of this publication may be reproduced, distributed, or transmitted in any form or by any means

WEEKLY SELF-ASSESSMENT 7 – – (COMPLETE/SHARE FOLLOWING)

Rate your SLEEP quality this week 1-10: _____   Rate your HEALTHY EATING this week 1-10: _____

Rate your EXERCISE/PHYSICAL ACTIVITY this week 1-10: _____

What's been your "BIGGEST STRUGGLE" over this past week?

On a scale of (1-to-10), rate this week's "struggle": (NOT BAD 1 - 2 - 3 - 4 - 5 - 6 - 7 - 8 - 9 - 10 WORST EVER)

What's the "BEST THING" you did or that happened to you this past week?

On a scale of (1-to-10), rate this week's "best thing": (NOT GREAT 1 - 2 - 3 - 4 - 5 - 6 - 7 - 8 - 9 - 10 BEST EVER)

What's the "MOST IMPORTANT THING YOU SHOULD BE DOING" this upcoming week?

On a scale of (1-to-10), rate how important it is to do "this thing": (NOT 1 - 2 - 3 - 4 - 5 - 6 - 7 - 8 - 9 – 10 VERY)

What would you rate your motivation this week? (NONE 1 - 2 - 3 - 4 - 5 - 6 - 7 - 8 - 9 – 10 TONS)

What would you rate your week overall? (ROUGH 1 - 2 - 3 - 4 - 5 - 6 - 7 - 8 - 9 – 10 AWESOME)

Was this past week better than the week before?   (YES) - (NO) - (SAME)

Finally, for every question you rated less than a 10, go back and ask yourself, "What made it less than a 10?" Then ask yourself, "What would it take for me to rate that question an 8+?" (These answers identify something we need to work on and what we need to do to fix it.)

Copyright © 2018 Michael E. Esser All rights reserved.
No part of this publication may be reproduced, distributed, or transmitted in any form or by any means

THOUGHT EXERCISES - SESSION 7: STAGES CHANGE/MAKING NEW HABITS

GOALS

- Our goal is to begin to adopt new/renewed healthy behaviors that move us away from addiction/criminal behaviors, while ending/removing any unhealthy ones that have been keeping us subject to that addiction and ruining our lives. We do this through the process of change.

- Begin to focus on the core skills we'll need to truly change; challenging our thoughts, new social/relationship skills, and new social/community skills.

- Begin to better understand the process of change, and its phases/stages, so that we can identify where we are in the process and where we can expect to be next.

- NOTE: *There are no time limits on these phases/stages. We all move through them at our own pace and no one can predict how long you'll be in any phases/stage. The more focused we are, the more we'll be ready to move towards the change we desire. Also, these phases/stages are not linear, and it is possible to move in any direction, at any time depending on your thoughts and actions at the time.*

DEFINITIONS

We discuss three phases to describe the process we're going through as we begin to make changes in our lives. In addition, we'll use Carlo C. DiClemente and J. O. Prochaska's, five-stage model of change to help us better understand addiction and the process of change. These include:

PRE-CONTEMPLATION: In this stage we are oblivious that we even have a problem or that anything is going on in our lives.

THE CHALLENGE PHASE

Copyright © 2018 Michael E. Esser All rights reserved.
No part of this publication may be reproduced, distributed, or transmitted in any form or by any means

It is in this phase that we begin challenging ourselves to begin to investigate what it is that we are having a problem with. It's here that we are going to have to begin to take a few healthy risks and begin to open ourselves up to the possibilities of a problem. In this phase, we are gathering information and when we are ready to commit to the changes needed, we're ready to move on to the pledge stage.

CONTEMPLATION: In this phase, we start seeing signs that there is a problem and begin to seek out more information.

PREPARATION: Once we've decided that we do need to make a change to the way we're living and the people, places, and things that are causing us so many problems, we begin to put in place the things we'll need. Searching for meetings, doing recovery related searches, deleting phone numbers and unfriending people on Facebook, etc.

THE PLEDGE PHASE

It is in this phase that we'll have gathered enough information and spent enough time searching ourselves that we'll be able to truly commit to moving forward with our change goals. We will start sharing a little more about ourselves than we might be used to and leave the door open to hear the sometimes hard to swallow feedback. Here we are continuing to open up more and starting to replace bad/old choices with new/healthier ones. It's here that we spend a significant amount of time understanding, growing, and beginning to get stronger and happier.

ACTION: In this stage, we make the first step towards change. We begin to reduce use, change where we go and who we hang out with, we're focused on the goal of changing and actively doing the things we need to make it happen.

THE OWNERSHIP PHASE

Copyright © 2018 Michael E. Esser All rights reserved.
No part of this publication may be reproduced, distributed, or transmitted in any form or by any means

In this phase we have made the changes, have seen the proof in our daily lives, and have the desire to maintain this homeostasis, or balance in our lives. It is in this phase that we start to grow beyond our addiction and other areas of our life begin to be explored as we venture out. Our confidence in our ability to better handle risky situations is strong and we proved to ourselves that we have truly changed as a person.

> **MAINTENANCE**: It is in this stage that we find homeostasis, or a balance in life in which our addiction is no longer part of our active lives. It has been some time since we last used or took part in that thing that has caused us so much pain. We are working, paying bills, happy for the most part, and working towards personal growth beyond our addiction.

RELAPSE

This additional stage is outside the three phases, but included because it is something that most people will most likely experience at some point during this process. Note: A lapse is a single use that we recover from, learn a lesson and get back on track. A relapse is a return to our old ways and how we acted and thought before we started this process.

APPLICATION TO ADDICTION

In our lives, we exist in the *pre-contemplation stage of change* when we have no idea, no clue that we even have a problem. We don't see the signs, we are in denial and we make excuses and don't want to change because we don't honestly see anything wrong with what we are doing.

It isn't until something happens, and we get in trouble, a fight, get arrested or some negative event takes place that we are even able to see and/or believe that there might be a problem that we need to address. It is in this catalyst type event that we begin to start looking for answers and move into the *challenge phase* as we begin to challenge our thoughts, beliefs, and understanding of our worlds.

Copyright © 2018 Michael E. Esser All rights reserved.
No part of this publication may be reproduced, distributed, or transmitted in any form or by any means

Here, we find ourselves in what is called the *contemplation stage of change.* It is now that we begin to see that something is wrong and at this point may or may not know exactly what it is, or if we even want to change it. It is in this consideration or contemplation that, *if* we want to change, we keep moving forward because now we need answers.

It is also during this information gathering stage that our concerns about ourselves may begin to include assessing how we've affected our family and their well-being, our relationships with our friends, and our place in society. Use this as a motivator.

Now at some point, when we have had enough of the problem being a constant presence in our life, it is then that we will naturally move forward into the *preparation stage of change*. Here we begin making plans and putting in place the tools and resources we need to help make the change we seek successfully happen. We will seek out helpful material/self-assessment tools, like this workbook, maybe call a counseling agency, find when and where the AA/NA meetings are, start talking to family and friends, etc.

From here, our next move is into the *pledge phase* or the *action stage of change.* We make this move the moment we take our actual first steps towards our goal. It begins the second we decide to quit, when attend our first meeting, when we start doing the things we need to do to remove this thing from our lives.

At this point, we'll also start setting goals for ourselves. These goals are meant to be our commitment or pledge to ourselves and what we are journeying towards. It's why we are not going to give up when things get tough and it's what is going to make it irrational for us to just return to our old ways. It is our clearly defined goal(s) that will help keep us on the right path and allow us to self-correct our course when we try to stray from it.

It is not going to be easy for most of us and we will have lapses in judgement and that is okay. We just need to stay committed to heading in the right direction that we've decided for ourselves, our loved ones, and our community. Continuing to seek help and self-reflect, continuing to have conversations with your healthy supporters, begin to develop healthy coping skills and work towards telling yourself nothing but positive things will help to keep you in this action stage. (All things we'll continue working on throughout this workbook.)

Copyright © 2018 Michael E. Esser All rights reserved.
No part of this publication may be reproduced, distributed, or transmitted in any form or by any means

Remember, when you're on your journey use the tools you have around you and keep your eyes and ears open for new tools that will be crossing your path. When something you didn't plan for happens, face that adversity with determination and don't simply give up because the journey became hard or because your initial plan didn't work out as perfectly planned. Don't stop and instead stay focused on your goal prepared to adapt again if you need.

When you do reach your goal and you have achieved a long period of relief from the addiction, keep your eyes and ears out for any other changes you may want or need to make as you continue to improve your life even further. It is in this place of accomplishment that we then begin the *ownership phase* of our lives/change. Here we have won more battles than we've lost and are beginning to share our story with the world.

We have a substantial amount of "clean time" under our belt and are not only talking the talk, but walking the walk. It is here that you are vested in yourself to the point that you won't risk all that you have worked to build, at least without a fight. Here you've begun to feel the reward of your commitment to change and don't want to look back. This is called the *maintenance stage of change* and it is the return to a sense of balance or homeostasis.

Note that when it comes to the "relapse" element of this process, know that it happens, and the goal is to learn from each one, if any. Think about:

- What you don't like about your lapse/relapse?

- What benefit did the lapse have on your life/goals overall? The costs?

Remember, "lapsing/relapsing" might set you back into the contemplation, preparation, and/or the action stage of change for this particular problem, but remember what got you through once before and can again. Now use that knowledge to return life back to where you were before the lapse/relapse.

NOW THAT WE'VE LEARNED ABOUT THE PHASES/STAGES OF CHANGE, WHICH PHASE/STAGE DO YOU FEEL YOU ARE IN RIGHT NOW? (SHARE YOUR RESPONSE)

WHERE ARE YOU ON THE READINESS SCALE?

(NO MOTIVATION) = 1 - 2 - 3 - 4 - 5 - 6 - 7 - 8 - 9 - 10 = (COMPLETELY MOTIVATED)

Copyright © 2018 Michael E. Esser All rights reserved.
No part of this publication may be reproduced, distributed, or transmitted in any form or by any means

Now ask yourself, "Why is my motivation where it is?"

"Why am I a five and not a nine?" and "What would it take to get me to that nine?" or "Why am I a ten?" and "What has me so motivated?"

Identifying what would increase your motivation gives you an idea of what you need to work on. Identifying why you are so motivated at this point gives you a clear view of what you value and see as important.

A straightforward way to get started in correcting these mental roadblocks is to evaluate what you really want using **WDEP** or:

- What do you really **WANT** when it comes to your addiction/charge/life?

- What are you **DOING** right now to get this goal?

- **EVALUATE** if what you're doing enough to get it? *YES OR NO (Circle)*

- If not, then what's your **PLAN**?

Source: https://www.apa.org

ARE THERE ROADBLOCKS KEEPING YOU FROM CHANGING?

Sometimes we have mental roadblocks that have made their way into our lives and they keep us from being able to change and might just have us down right refusing to change. If you are saying any of the following things to yourself, it's a problem and we need to put a plan in place to remove them.

- *I've tried before, and it didn't work.*

- *I've just always been this way. It's not worth the effort to change.*

- *Everyone around me does it, so why can't I?*

- *I don't need change, I don't like change; it's uncomfortable.*

SHARE YOUR RESPONSES WITH THE GROUP

Copyright © 2018 Michael E. Esser All rights reserved.

No part of this publication may be reproduced, distributed, or transmitted in any form or by any means

WEEKLY SELF-ASSESSMENT 8 – (COMPLETE/SHARE FOLLOWING)

Rate your SLEEP quality this week 1-10: _____ Rate your HEALTHY EATING this week 1-10: _____

Rate your EXERCISE/PHYSICAL ACTIVITY this week 1-10: _____

What's been your "BIGGEST STRUGGLE" over this past week?
On a scale of (1-to-10), rate this week's "struggle": (NOT BAD 1 - 2 - 3 - 4 - 5 - 6 - 7 - 8 - 9 - 10 WORST EVER)
What's the "BEST THING" you did or that happened to you this past week?
On a scale of (1-to-10), rate this week's "best thing": (NOT GREAT 1 - 2 - 3 - 4 - 5 - 6 - 7 - 8 - 9 - 10 BEST EVER)
What's the "MOST IMPORTANT THING YOU SHOULD BE DOING" this upcoming week?
On a scale of (1-to-10), rate how important it is to do "this thing": (NOT 1 - 2 - 3 - 4 - 5 - 6 - 7 - 8 - 9 – 10 VERY)
What would you rate your motivation this week? (NONE 1 - 2 - 3 - 4 - 5 - 6 - 7 - 8 - 9 – 10 TONS)
What would you rate your week overall? (ROUGH 1 - 2 - 3 - 4 - 5 - 6 - 7 - 8 - 9 – 10 AWESOME)
Was this past week better than the week before?   (YES) - (NO) - (SAME)
Finally, for every question you rated less than a 10, go back and ask yourself, "What made it less than a 10?" Then ask yourself, "What would it take for me to rate that question an 8+?" (These answers identify something we need to work on and what we need to do to fix it.)

Copyright © 2018 Michael E. Esser All rights reserved.
No part of this publication may be reproduced, distributed, or transmitted in any form or by any means

THOUGHT EXERCISES - SESSION 8: REVIEW SESSIONS 1-7 + COPING SKILL

Going back and reviewing the past few sessions is something we'll do throughout this workbook. *To do this, you will go back and review each session and answer the following questions or summary requests.*

1. WHAT'S SOMETHING FROM SESSION 1 THAT HAS STUCK WITH YOU?

_____

(COMPLETE THE FOLLOWING SENTENCE IN THE SPACE PROVIDED)

"IN SESSION ONE WE LEARNED... _____

_____

_____."

2. WHAT'S SOMETHING FROM SESSION 2 THAT HAS STUCK WITH YOU?

_____

"IN SESSION TWO WE LEARNED... _____

_____

_____."

3. WHAT'S SOMETHING FROM SESSION 3 THAT HAS STUCK WITH YOU?

_____

"IN SESSION THREE WE LEARNED... _____

_____

_____."

4. WHAT'S SOMETHING FROM SESSION 4 THAT HAS STUCK WITH YOU?

_____

"IN SESSION FOUR WE LEARNED... _____

_____

_____."

Copyright © 2018 Michael E. Esser All rights reserved.
No part of this publication may be reproduced, distributed, or transmitted in any form or by any means

5. WHAT'S SOMETHING FROM SESSION 5 THAT HAS STUCK WITH YOU?

_____

(COMPLETE THE FOLLOWING SENTENCE IN THE SPACE PROVIDED)

"IN SESSION FIVE WE LEARNED... _____

_____

_____."

6. WHAT'S SOMETHING FROM SESSION 6 THAT HAS STUCK WITH YOU?

_____

"IN SESSION SIX WE LEARNED... _____

_____

_____."

7. WHAT'S SOMETHING FROM SESSION 7 THAT HAS STUCK WITH YOU?

_____

"IN SESSION SEVEN WE LEARNED... _____

_____

_____."

COPING SKILLS:

Distract yourself; have a conversation with someone, clean something, focus on a hobby, watch TV, listen to radio, take a walk, or do a word search. **Pro**: Great short-term relief, gives you a break during crisis

Challenge your thoughts; write down all the negative thoughts you're having and then list the reasons they're not true, look for the positive. **Pro**: Can change negative habits

Access the giver in you; help someone else by volunteering, do something nice for no reason, smile and count the smiles you influence in others. **Pro**: Let's us find value in the little things and that everyone has significance.

END OF PHASE II – CONTINUE TO PHASE I OR COMPLETE FINALS

Copyright © 2018 Michael E. Esser All rights reserved.
No part of this publication may be reproduced, distributed, or transmitted in any form or by any means

LEVEL I TREATMENT - SESSIONS 1-18 + FINALS (36 HOURS)

WEEKLY SELF-ASSESSMENT 9 – (COMPLETE/SHARE FOLLOWING)

Rate your SLEEP quality this week 1-10: _____ Rate your HEALTHY EATING this week 1-10: _____

Rate your EXERCISE/PHYSICAL ACTIVITY this week 1-10: _____

What's been your "BIGGEST STRUGGLE" over this past week?
On a scale of (1-to-10), rate this week's "struggle": (NOT BAD 1 - 2 - 3 - 4 - 5 - 6 - 7 - 8 - 9 - 10 WORST EVER)
What's the "BEST THING" you did or that happened to you this past week?
On a scale of (1-to-10), rate this week's "best thing": (NOT GREAT 1 - 2 - 3 - 4 - 5 - 6 - 7 - 8 - 9 - 10 BEST EVER)
What's the "MOST IMPORTANT THING YOU SHOULD BE DOING" this upcoming week?
On a scale of (1-to-10), rate how important it is to do "this thing": (NOT 1 - 2 - 3 - 4 - 5 - 6 - 7 - 8 - 9 – 10 VERY)
What would you rate your motivation this week? (NONE 1 - 2 - 3 - 4 - 5 - 6 - 7 - 8 - 9 – 10 TONS)
What would you rate your week overall? (ROUGH 1 - 2 - 3 - 4 - 5 - 6 - 7 - 8 - 9 – 10 AWESOME)
Was this past week better than the week before?   (YES) - (NO) - (SAME)
Finally, for every question you rated less than a 10, go back and ask yourself, "What made it less than a 10?" Then ask yourself, "What would it take for me to rate that question an 8+?" (These answers identify something we need to work on and what we need to do to fix it.)

Copyright © 2018 Michael E. Esser All rights reserved.
No part of this publication may be reproduced, distributed, or transmitted in any form or by any means

THOUGHT EXERCISES - SESSION 9: SLEEP, NUTRITION, AND EXERCISE BENEFITS

We spend a majority of our time focused on our recovery, bettering our family, and working to provide. The idea that we are working so hard to overcome addiction and the unhealthy habits that cripple our daily routine is not only praiseworthy, but admirable. Unfortunately, this usually leaves an empty space in our world that needs to be filled with something positive and that means developing encouraging and healthy friendships, finding ways to improve the quality time you spend with the family, and discovering a natural source for the renewed energy we need to accomplish all the important things that are on our plate these days.

If we are going to truly be healthy individuals, we need to take holistic approach to our health. We need to have plans in place to take care of the only mind and body we have, or are ever going to get – barring the commercialization of cloning.

To function the way we need, our bodies must get enough quality sleep, sufficient nutrients, and adequate exercise. (Add *love* and *learning* to the list and that makes up the main pillars of healthy living.) Learning is what we've been doing throughout this entire workbook and hopefully we find ourselves loving life and those around us more as we continue to get healthier over time.

It's in paying attention to these elements of our health that we also see our body optimize its production of neurons. Neurons are the cells in our bodies that carry electrical impulses to the brain and the basic units of our nervous systems. It is in this production, called "neurogenesis" or the growth of new brain cells, that we promote the system functions that allows us to keep our minds as we get older.

SLEEP FACTS/BENEFITS

- Sleep happens in 90-minute cycles on average.

- It's during these 90-minute cycles that HGH is released, or about an hour into sleep. HGH is the naturally occurring growth hormone of humans. Experts estimate up to 75% of our human growth hormone is released during sleep.

- Planning to sleep in 90-minute units, or 3 hours, 4.5 hours, 6 hours, and so on allows our bodies to complete its natural cycles. Interrupting these

Copyright © 2018 Michael E. Esser All rights reserved.
No part of this publication may be reproduced, distributed, or transmitted in any form or by any means

cycles with alarm clocks set to wake us at an inappropriate or unplanned hour may cause us to feel unrested or unfulfilled with our sleep.

- Also, when we sleep our brain removes the toxins it builds up throughout the day. The brain is not part of the rest of the bodies "toxin removal" system and puts off this "cleaning" until we sleep.

NUTRITION

- What we put into our body is the fuel we use to run all our systems – bad in, bad out – its simple math.

- When we eat a balanced diet filled with as much locally source foods as possible we thrive.

- Having as much as 3-5 meals a day, in a 9-12-hour window, that consist of a palm-sized portion of protein, a fist-sized portion of a complex carb, and a fist-sized portion of fiber-rich vegetables is the simple rule of thumb.

- Snacking on healthy fats like avocado, nuts, or coconut oils is encouraged.

- Always try to pair a protein with your carbs so that to promote balance in how your body processes the fuel.

- Remember to drink plenty of water to help keep your system hydrated.

EXERCISE

At first this doesn't need to be difficult. You don't need to do anything more than start taking a walk sometime during the day for around 15-20 minutes.

After that, think about your body in sections; your legs and abs, your chest and shoulders, and your arms and back. Now, everyday stretch those parts of your body out for a few minutes and do a simple workout routine of body squats, toe touches, and pushups.

Once you feel stronger and want more of a challenge, you can seek out anyone of thousands of other workouts to do from there on.

WHAT DO YOU DO FOR YOUR HEALTH? WHAT IS YOUR DAILY ROUTINE? SHARE

Copyright © 2018 Michael E. Esser All rights reserved.
No part of this publication may be reproduced, distributed, or transmitted in any form or by any means

WEEKLY SELF-ASSESSMENT 10 – (COMPLETE/SHARE FOLLOWING)

Rate your SLEEP quality this week 1-10: _____   Rate your HEALTHY EATING this week 1-10: _____

Rate your EXERCISE/PHYSICAL ACTIVITY this week 1-10: _____

What's been your "BIGGEST STRUGGLE" over this past week?
On a scale of (1-to-10), rate this week's "struggle": (NOT BAD 1 - 2 - 3 - 4 - 5 - 6 - 7 - 8 - 9 - 10 WORST EVER)
What's the "BEST THING" you did or that happened to you this past week?
On a scale of (1-to-10), rate this week's "best thing": (NOT GREAT 1 - 2 - 3 - 4 - 5 - 6 - 7 - 8 - 9 - 10 BEST EVER)
What's the "MOST IMPORTANT THING YOU SHOULD BE DOING" this upcoming week?
On a scale of (1-to-10), rate how important it is to do "this thing": (NOT 1 - 2 - 3 - 4 - 5 - 6 - 7 - 8 - 9 – 10 VERY)
What would you rate your motivation this week? (NONE 1 - 2 - 3 - 4 - 5 - 6 - 7 - 8 - 9 – 10 TONS)
What would you rate your week overall? (ROUGH 1 - 2 - 3 - 4 - 5 - 6 - 7 - 8 - 9 – 10 AWESOME)
Was this past week better than the week before?   (YES) - (NO) - (SAME)
Finally, for every question you rated less than a 10, go back and ask yourself, "What made it less than a 10?" Then ask yourself, "What would it take for me to rate that question an 8+?" (These answers identify something we need to work on and what we need to do to fix it.)

Copyright © 2018 Michael E. Esser All rights reserved.

No part of this publication may be reproduced, distributed, or transmitted in any form or by any means

THOUGHT EXERCISES -SESSION 10: BOUNDARIES/NEGATIVE SELF-TALK

A personal boundary is our way of communicating to the world, "this is my limit." It's the separation between our energy and the energy of everything and everyone around us.

Maintaining our boundary is not to be confused with putting up a defensive wall. It's more of a tool for protecting a sense of who we are, so that we don't give too much of ourselves a way to the rest of the world.

Boundaries are important to prevent burnout and over-extending ourselves. You need boundaries to maintain mental peace. Beyond the physical safety aspect of boundaries, we are also less likely to store-up guilt or resentment, both towards ourselves or others, that can manifest into symptoms like stress or sleep issues.

Connecting with our boundaries help us build our self-esteem and raise our energy level. If we don't have healthy boundaries in place and we're feeling drained, we may fall into a pattern of latching on to someone else – like a parasite – just to maintain our own energy levels. We can become codependent.

HERE'S HOW TO BEGIN TO SET YOUR BOUNDARIES

• Practice saying "no" instead of just saying "yes" and over-committing yourself. Decide what you really want to do or not do and say "no." Ex. "Thank you but, I don't like the bar scene anymore."

• Be mindful. Guilty thoughts can circulate in your mind. Stop this thinking! Ex. "Stop! I am worthy. I am not a screw up, I'm smart."

• Speak up from a compassionate place. Let people know how you feel about how their actions or words affect you. Ex. "I stress out when we yell."

• Always have a way out of any conversation with someone overstepping. Politely interject that you need to return to the task you were doing when the conversation began. Ex. "I'm sorry, I have to get back to shopping."

• Plan regular "you" time. You need to be able to take care of your own needs. Basically, when you respect yourself, it teaches others to respect you as well. Ex. "I can't do that today. I am going to get my hair cut and take a nap."

Copyright © 2018 Michael E. Esser All rights reserved.
No part of this publication may be reproduced, distributed, or transmitted in any form or by any means

• be sure to commit to your diet, fitness, and bedtime. What you eat is the source of all your energy. Put good stuff in, get good out. Moving your body with purpose every day means improved circulation and reduced stress. Finally, sleep is a vital part of feeling refreshed and strong, which happens to be the best place to be when it comes to making good decisions.

PUTTING THE SPOTLIGHT ON NEGATIVE SELF-TALK

Where does your GUILT/STRESS/BOREDOM/ETC. come from?

MAKE A "WHAT STRESSES YOU OUT?" LIST (EX: LIES, BILLS, MONEY...)

We were taught that these events/situations where the source of what made us feel guilty/stressed/bored, BUT THEY'RE NOT. It's our NEGATIVE SELF-TALK or WHAT WE TELL OURSELVES ABOUT THESE THINGS that makes us feel those ways.

If we learn to CONTROL OUR SELF-TALK then we'll CONTROL OUR POINT OF VIEW.

WHAT IS YOUR NATURAL WAY OF DEALING WITH STRESS? (CRY, EAT, USE, DRINK, BOTTLE UP, ZONE OUT, ETC.)

Challenge each item listed. Is there another way? Try asking someone how they'd respond to that same situation and if they think you can get over it. What advice would you give a friend? Now, write the best answers next to your first thought.

SHARE YOUR RESPONSES WITH THE GROUP

Copyright © 2018 Michael E. Esser All rights reserved.
No part of this publication may be reproduced, distributed, or transmitted in any form or by any means

WEEKLY SELF-ASSESSMENT 11 – _(COMPLETE/SHARE FOLLOWING)_

Rate your SLEEP quality this week 1-10: _____ Rate your HEALTHY EATING this week 1-10: _____

Rate your EXERCISE/PHYSICAL ACTIVITY this week 1-10: _____

What's been your "BIGGEST STRUGGLE" over this past week?
On a scale of (1-to-10), rate this week's "struggle": (NOT BAD 1 - 2 - 3 - 4 - 5 - 6 - 7 - 8 - 9 - 10 WORST EVER)
What's the "BEST THING" you did or that happened to you this past week?
On a scale of (1-to-10), rate this week's "best thing": (NOT GREAT 1 - 2 - 3 - 4 - 5 - 6 - 7 - 8 - 9 - 10 BEST EVER)
What's the "MOST IMPORTANT THING YOU SHOULD BE DOING" this upcoming week?
On a scale of (1-to-10), rate how important it is to do "this thing": (NOT 1 - 2 - 3 - 4 - 5 - 6 - 7 - 8 - 9 – 10 VERY)
What would you rate your motivation this week? (NONE 1 - 2 - 3 - 4 - 5 - 6 - 7 - 8 - 9 – 10 TONS)
What would you rate your week overall? (ROUGH 1 - 2 - 3 - 4 - 5 - 6 - 7 - 8 - 9 – 10 AWESOME)
Was this past week better than the week before?   (YES) - (NO) - (SAME)
Finally, for every question you rated less than a 10, go back and ask yourself, "What made it less than a 10?" Then ask yourself, "What would it take for me to rate that question an 8+?" (These answers identify something we need to work on and what we need to do to fix it.)

Copyright © 2018 Michael E. Esser All rights reserved.

No part of this publication may be reproduced, distributed, or transmitted in any form or by any means

THOUGHT EXERCISES -SESSION 11: RELAPSE/CRAVING V. URGE/TRIGGERS

RELAPSE AND RECIDIVISM

Relapse/recidivism prevention is why we seek help. At this point, most of us have already tried to quit or stop on our own and now seek a better solution. It's the tendency to relapse to a previous behavior like drug use or illegal activity.

MAIN IDEAS IN RELAPSE/RECIDIVISM PREVENTION

Relapse/recidivism begins when you start "THINKING" about using/committing a crime or when you "ACCIDENTALLY" find yourself in an environment or with people where there's drugs/alcohol or criminal/activity that you can participate in.

Relapse/recidivism prevention consists of changing our existing life and creating a new life where it is easier to not use or do that thing that got us in trouble. We do this by being completely honest; asking for help; paying attention to our self-care; and sticking to the plans we set for ourselves. Relapse happens gradually and in stages that include: Emotional, Mental, and Physical Relapse.

EMOTIONAL RELAPSE

We're not thinking about relapse and still remember the last time we did, but the way we're thinking, and acting is setting us up and denial is letting it happen.

In emotional relapse, we start bottling up emotions; isolating ourselves; 3) stop sharing or stop going to meetings altogether; start focusing on others and stop taking care of ourselves as well as we were.

MENTAL RELAPSE

Mental relapse is like a civil war in your mind. Some part of us wants it and the rest does not. As the war continues our strength to hold out gets weaker and we may succumb just to escape the turmoil. This is where we start having cravings and start thinking about old people, laces, and things. We start planning to relapse and come up with the ways we'll justify it and lie about it to ourselves and others.

PHYSICAL RELAPSE

Physical relapse happens when we start using again. Some researchers divide physical relapse into a "lapse" (the initial drink or drug use) and a "relapse" (a return to uncontrolled using). Most physical relapses are relapses of opportunity.

Copyright © 2018 Michael E. Esser All rights reserved.

No part of this publication may be reproduced, distributed, or transmitted in any form or by any means

POST-ACUTE WITHDRAWAL

After we've detoxified our body of the substances, we need to be aware of something called post-acute withdrawal, or PAWS, as it is a common cause of relapse. What we know as withdrawal is mostly associated with physical symptoms, but PAWS is different in that it's mostly associated with psychological and emotional symptoms and are likely to be similar for most addictions.

These symptoms can include; mood swings, anxiety, irritability, inconstant energy, low interest, troubles concentrating, and sleep issues.

One of the most important things to know about PAWS is that they can last up to 2 years, with symptoms coming and going for no logical reason.

Source: https://www.ncbi.nlm.nih.gov

CRAVING (THOUGHT) V. URGE (ACTION)

SIMPLE DEFINITION: A craving is when you start thinking about ice cream. An urge is when you're getting in the car to go solve that urge with a double scoop.

KEEP TRIGGERS AND CRAVINGS IN CHECK

Your recovery doesn't end at getting sober. Your brain still needs time to recover and rebuild connections that changed while you were addicted. During this rebuild, drug cravings can be intense. You can support your continued recovery by avoiding people, places, and situations that trigger your urge to use:

• Step away from your friends who use.

• Avoid bars and clubs.

• Be upfront about your history of drug use when seeking medical treatment.

• Use caution with prescription drugs.

WRITE DOWN YOUR BIGGEST TRIGGERS

COPING WITH DRUG CRAVINGS

Sometimes craving cannot be avoided, and it is necessary to find a way to cope:

• Get involved in a distracting activity.

Copyright © 2018 Michael E. Esser All rights reserved.
No part of this publication may be reproduced, distributed, or transmitted in any form or by any means

- Talk it through.

- Urge surf.

- Challenge and change your thoughts.

TELL YOURSELF TO H.A.L.T. THEN, ASK YOURSELF...

"Am I **H**ungry, **A**ngry **L**onely or **T**ired?" Then, address that feeling accordingly. Eat, talk about problem, talk to someone, or get some rest.

BIG LIST OF HELPFUL TIPS AND TRICKS FOR SUCCESSFUL CHANGE

Follow a routine / stay on a schedule / stay busy / find a good hobby / get a job

Call someone when you feel triggered or like relapsing / talk to people

Give yourself enough time to show up to things early

Be honest / be responsible / be thankful

Disassociate with old people / ditch old people and old habits

Do exercise / do push-ups when triggered

Set goals / continuously be setting new goals / realistic goals / Track saved money

Identify and rely on your higher power

Know what motivates you / admit your weakness / know you're worth it

Stay focused / stay mindful / be of a strong mind / decide to be different

Focus on persevering / think "nothing is going to stop me"

Have confidence in yourself / care about yourself

Change your mindset / make use "not an option"/ don't beat yourself up

It's on your time / one day at a time / Just keep doing the next right thing

BECAUSE WE'RE REPLACING OLD BAD BEHAVIORS WITH NEW HEALTHY ONES, IDENTIFY AT LEAST TWO HOBBY YOU ARE INTERESTED IN.

*SHARE YOUR HOBBIE AND WHY YOU LIKE IT WITH THE GROUP

Copyright © 2018 Michael E. Esser All rights reserved.
No part of this publication may be reproduced, distributed, or transmitted in any form or by any means

WEEKLY SELF-ASSESSMENT 12 – (COMPLETE/SHARE FOLLOWING)

Rate your SLEEP quality this week 1-10: _____ Rate your HEALTHY EATING this week 1-10: _____

Rate your EXERCISE/PHYSICAL ACTIVITY this week 1-10: _____

What's been your "BIGGEST STRUGGLE" over this past week?

On a scale of (1-to-10), rate this week's "struggle": (NOT BAD 1 - 2 - 3 - 4 - 5 - 6 - 7 - 8 - 9 - 10 WORST EVER)

What's the "BEST THING" you did or that happened to you this past week?

On a scale of (1-to-10), rate this week's "best thing": (NOT GREAT 1 - 2 - 3 - 4 - 5 - 6 - 7 - 8 - 9 - 10 BEST EVER)

What's the "MOST IMPORTANT THING YOU SHOULD BE DOING" this upcoming week?

On a scale of (1-to-10), rate how important it is to do "this thing": (NOT 1 - 2 - 3 - 4 - 5 - 6 - 7 - 8 - 9 – 10 VERY)

What would you rate your motivation this week? (NONE 1 - 2 - 3 - 4 - 5 - 6 - 7 - 8 - 9 – 10 TONS)

What would you rate your week overall? (ROUGH 1 - 2 - 3 - 4 - 5 - 6 - 7 - 8 - 9 – 10 AWESOME)

Was this past week better than the week before?   (YES) - (NO) - (SAME)

Finally, for every question you rated less than a 10, go back and ask yourself, "What made it less than a 10?" Then ask yourself, "What would it take for me to rate that question an 8+?" (These answers identify something we need to work on and what we need to do to fix it.)

Copyright © 2018 Michael E. Esser All rights reserved.
No part of this publication may be reproduced, distributed, or transmitted in any form or by any means

THOUGHT EXERCISES -SESSION 12: BUILDING SUPPORT SYSTEM/AFFIRMATIONS

WHAT DOES IT MEAN TO HAVE A MEANINGFUL LIFE?

One way you can support a healthy lifestyle and healthy prosocial changes is by having activities and interests that provide meaning to your life. It's important to be involved in things that you enjoy and make you feel needed.

When your life is filled with rewarding activities and a sense of purpose, your "addictions" or unhealthy activities will tend to lose their appeal.

- Find your passion and get involved in that community.

- Set meaningful goals and put systems in place to accomplish them.

- Look after your health. Regular exercise, adequate sleep, and healthy eating habits help you keep your energy levels up and your stress levels down. The more you can stay healthy and feel good, the easier it will be to stay on track.

- Pick up a new hobby.

- Adopt a pet.

This list is not conclusive, but for the sake of this discussion should include...

- SURROUNDING YOURSELF WITH A HEALTHY SUPPORT SYSTEM!

WHAT IS A HEALTHY SUPPORT NETWORK?

Basically, a healthy support network consists of a balanced mix of the following:

- **MENTORS/ROLE MODELS:** those that show by example your desired behaviors

- **HEALTHY PEERS:** new or existing healthy individuals

- **SUPPORTIVE FAMILY MEMEBERS:** positive family members that support you

- **SKILLED HELP**: counselors, probation officer, pastor, etc. trained individuals

WHO IS IN YOUR HEALTHY SUPPORT NETWORK?

Copyright © 2018 Michael E. Esser All rights reserved.
No part of this publication may be reproduced, distributed, or transmitted in any form or by any means

POSITIVE SELF-AFFIRMATIONS

Affirmations are positive, specific statements that help you to overcome self-sabotaging, negative thoughts. They help you visualize, and believe in, what you're affirming to yourself, helping you to make positive changes to your life and career.

WHY AFFIRMATIONS DON'T WORK:

- Your affirmation is unrealistic, and your conscious mind rejects it.

- Affirmation isn't specific enough, so your conscious mind rejects it.

- You don't take enough action. There is no magic pill or easy way out.

- No consistency. It's only overtime that we improve.

PICKING A TENSE:

- "I am…" are cool but these statements can be rejected, if not believable

- "I will be…" are a better alternative because they promote a future goal

- "I have the knowledge/strength to…" are best because they promote self

IMPLEMENTING YOUR AFFIRMATIONS:

- Recite before bed and when you wake up – when your mind is best "primed."

- Write your affirmations down in a notebook to carry around with you.

- Write them on "post it" notes so you can place them all over your home.

SEVEN COMMON EXAMPLES OF HEALTHY POSITIVE SELF-AFFIRMATIONS:

1) *I can achieve greatness.* By telling this to yourself and believing that you can achieve greatness, it will eventually turn into reality.

2) Today, I am brimming with energy and overflowing with joy. Joy starts from within not from outside of yourself. It also starts as soon as you rise. Make it habit to repeat this to yourself first thing.

3) *I love and accept myself for who I am.* Self-love is meant to be the purest and the highest form of love. When you love yourself, you automatically start appreciating and respecting yourself. If you have confidence and pride in what

Copyright © 2018 Michael E. Esser All rights reserved.
No part of this publication may be reproduced, distributed, or transmitted in any form or by any means

you do, you will begin to see yourself in a new light and be encouraged and inspired to do bigger and better things.

4) *My body is healthy; my mind is brilliant; my soul is tranquil.* A healthy body starts with a healthy mind and soul. You are conquering your illness and defeating it steadily each day.

5) *Today, I abandon my old habits and take up new, more positive ones.* Realize that any difficult times are only a short phase of life. It will all pass soon, along with your old habits, as you take in the new.

6) *Everything that is happening now is happening for my ultimate good.* You are at peace with all that has happened, is happening, and will happen. Your fears of tomorrow are simply melting away.

7) *I am the architect of my life; I build its foundation and choose its contents.* This is something that you should tell yourself when you wake up every morning. You can make anything of that day that you like because you are the architect of your own life.

COME UP WITH YOUR OWN POSITIVE SELF-AFFIRMATION AND/OR DRAW A PICTURE TO MATCH IT:

Copyright © 2018 Michael E. Esser All rights reserved.

No part of this publication may be reproduced, distributed, or transmitted in any form or by any means

WEEKLY SELF-ASSESSMENT 13 – _(COMPLETE/SHARE FOLLOWING)_

Rate your SLEEP quality this week 1-10: _____ Rate your HEALTHY EATING this week 1-10: _____

Rate your EXERCISE/PHYSICAL ACTIVITY this week 1-10: _____

What's been your "BIGGEST STRUGGLE" over this past week?
On a scale of (1-to-10), rate this week's "struggle": (NOT BAD 1 - 2 - 3 - 4 - 5 - 6 - 7 - 8 - 9 - 10 WORST EVER)
What's the "BEST THING" you did or that happened to you this past week?
On a scale of (1-to-10), rate this week's "best thing": (NOT GREAT 1 - 2 - 3 - 4 - 5 - 6 - 7 - 8 - 9 - 10 BEST EVER)
What's the "MOST IMPORTANT THING YOU SHOULD BE DOING" this upcoming week?
On a scale of (1-to-10), rate how important it is to do "this thing": (NOT 1 - 2 - 3 - 4 - 5 - 6 - 7 - 8 - 9 – 10 VERY)
What would you rate your motivation this week? (NONE 1 - 2 - 3 - 4 - 5 - 6 - 7 - 8 - 9 – 10 TONS)
What would you rate your week overall? (ROUGH 1 - 2 - 3 - 4 - 5 - 6 - 7 - 8 - 9 – 10 AWESOME)
Was this past week better than the week before?   (YES) - (NO) - (SAME)
**Finally, for every question you rated less than a 10, go back and ask yourself, "What made it less than a 10?" Then ask yourself, "What would it take for me to rate that question an 8+?" (These answers identify something we need to work on and what we need to do to fix it.)**

Copyright © 2018 Michael E. Esser All rights reserved.
No part of this publication may be reproduced, distributed, or transmitted in any form or by any means

THOUGHT EXERCISES - SESSION 13: GRIEF/HEALING/SELF-SOOTHING

GRIEF

For some, dealing with their addiction or possible criminal offense means having to deal with some form of grief that may have led to the use or crime. There are five stages of grief that were first suggested by Elisabeth Kübler-Ross in her 1969 book On Death and Dying.

These stages of grief and loss are:

1. **Denial and isolation**: "This isn't happening, this can't be happening."

2. **Anger and denial**: Not being ready our vulnerable core expresses anger/denial.

3. **Bargaining**: Feeling helpless we try to regain control with "If only" statements.

4. **Depression**: Two types, "sadness and regret" and "quiet preparation to let go."

5. **Acceptance**: Peace, withdrawal, and calm. This stage of grieving is a gift.

Grieving individuals don't necessarily need to go through these stages in order nor do they have to experience each stage. EVERYONE GRIEVES DIFFERENTLY. The mission with providing this information is to build your awareness and in that enlightenment, have more understanding about what you may be feeling.

UNHEALTHY COPING SKILLS

- Isolating yourself from others.

- Fighting your feelings.

- Getting stuck in anger, resentment, or blame.

- Making any major decisions right after the breakup.

- Coping with alcohol, drugs, or excessive food intake.

- Thoughts/acts of self-harm

- Thoughts/acts of harming someone else

IDENTIFY AN UNHEALTHY COPING SKILLS YOU'VE USED IN REAL LIFE:

Copyright © 2018 Michael E. Esser All rights reserved.

No part of this publication may be reproduced, distributed, or transmitted in any form or by any means

HEALTHY COPING SKILLS

- Be honest with yourself and accept feelings

- Understand it takes time

- Share your feelings

- Know grief doesn't last forever

- Spend time with those who support you.

- Find new friends or groups (if needed)

- Explore new interests to distract yourself (if needed)

- Participate in a community activities/volunteer

- Get rest, but not too much

IDENTIFY TWO HEALTHY COPING SKILLS YOU'D USE IN REAL LIFE:

HEALING

Life is series of ups and downs. The good news is it is possible to heal the emotional scars. Devising coping strategies that address these ups - anxiety, and downs – depression can help us to be a happier, healthier individual.

HEALING STRATEGIES

Keep a Journal

Its purpose is to allow you to get whatever is in your head out and onto a piece of paper. Also, note that you're not writing for anyone else but yourself so be free!

Benefits:

This gives you a place to begin to document your growth and any new understandings you come to.

Something you can come back to later as a way of learning from your past thoughts.

Copyright © 2018 Michael E. Esser All rights reserved.
No part of this publication may be reproduced, distributed, or transmitted in any form or by any means

A safe, private place to express your thoughts and feelings you're not ready to share. A place to let out your anger or stress but also your hopes and dreams.

Visualizing Exercises

The power of mental imaging and concentrating on the change you desire might just be the answer to your circumstances.

Benefits:

This can give you a useful mechanism that can help you begin to imagine distancing yourself from negative feelings, situations, or unhealthy people.

It can also be a very powerful tool for recreating encouraging or favorable memories.

This isn't a comprehensive list, by no means, but let these examples be something that can inspire you to seek out additional strategies.

MOOD-LIFTING TRICKS

1.   Cut the negativity

2.   Stop gossiping

3.   Stop people-pleasing

4.   Give up giving up

5.   Let go of that grudge (once and for all)

6.   Stop getting down on yourself

7.   Stop taking yourself so seriously

8.   Stop worrying about what others think

WHICH ONE OF THESE TRICKS WOULD YOU ACTUALLY USE IN YOU DAILY LIFE AND WHY?

Copyright © 2018 Michael E. Esser All rights reserved.
No part of this publication may be reproduced, distributed, or transmitted in any form or by any means

SELF-SOOTHING

Self-soothing is a state of calming that you accomplish on your own and it's typically achieved by either distracting yourself, shifting focus to the pros and cons of a situation, or simply improving the current moment.

It's in these strategies that we can short circuit our brains and help ourselves to begin to cope with any overwhelming negative emotions or intolerable situations. It does take a lot of practice, but as you get the hang of using these techniques, you will see your relationship to the negative emotions begin to change.

SELF-SOOTHING has to do with comforting, nurturing and being kind to yourself.

TRY SOOTHING YOUR FIVE SENSES:

VISION

Experience art. Look at the flowers. Go to a garden.

HEARING

Listen to soothing music or sounds of nature.

SMELL

Light a scented candle. Bake some cookies.

TASTE

Eat the cookies. Drink some fancy tea.

TOUCH

Take a bubble bath. Snuggle with a pet. Put on soft pajamas.

WHAT'S SOMETHING YOU DO TO LIFT YOUR MOOD AND SELF-SOOTH? IF NOTHING NOTABLE, PICK ONE OF THE OPTIONS PRESENTED THIS SESSION AND SHARE HOW THAT CHOICE COULD HELP YOU.

Copyright © 2018 Michael E. Esser All rights reserved.
No part of this publication may be reproduced, distributed, or transmitted in any form or by any means

WEEKLY SELF-ASSESSMENT 14 – (COMPLETE/SHARE FOLLOWING)

Rate your SLEEP quality this week 1-10: _____   Rate your HEALTHY EATING this week 1-10: _____

Rate your EXERCISE/PHYSICAL ACTIVITY this week 1-10: _____

What's been your "BIGGEST STRUGGLE" over this past week?

On a scale of (1-to-10), rate this week's "struggle": (NOT BAD 1 - 2 - 3 - 4 - 5 - 6 - 7 - 8 - 9 - 10 WORST EVER)

What's the "BEST THING" you did or that happened to you this past week?

On a scale of (1-to-10), rate this week's "best thing": (NOT GREAT 1 - 2 - 3 - 4 - 5 - 6 - 7 - 8 - 9 - 10 BEST EVER)

What's the "MOST IMPORTANT THING YOU SHOULD BE DOING" this upcoming week?

On a scale of (1-to-10), rate how important it is to do "this thing": (NOT 1 - 2 - 3 - 4 - 5 - 6 - 7 - 8 - 9 – 10 VERY)

What would you rate your motivation this week? (NONE 1 - 2 - 3 - 4 - 5 - 6 - 7 - 8 - 9 – 10 TONS)

What would you rate your week overall? (ROUGH 1 - 2 - 3 - 4 - 5 - 6 - 7 - 8 - 9 – 10 AWESOME)

Was this past week better than the week before?   (YES) - (NO) - (SAME)

Finally, for every question you rated less than a 10, go back and ask yourself, "What made it less than a 10?" Then ask yourself, "What would it take for me to rate that question an 8+?" (These answers identify something we need to work on and what we need to do to fix it.)

Copyright © 2018 Michael E. Esser All rights reserved.
No part of this publication may be reproduced, distributed, or transmitted in any form or by any means

THOUGHT EXERCISES - SESSION 14: ANGER MANAGEMENT

ANGER

Anger may be an unpleasant emotion to deal with, but it's a normal, healthy part of being human. If you express it in a healthy way, anger can serve as a powerful motivating force, but chronic anger can affect your relationships and can increase your risk of a reoffending/relapsing or even a heart-attack or stroke.

ANGER TYPES

General anger is a strong feeling of annoyance, displeasure, or hostility.

Passive Aggressive behavior takes many forms but can generally be described as a non-verbal aggression that is displayed through negative behaviors. It is where you are angry with someone but do not or cannot tell them. You don't say what you want.

Volatile Anger tends to be an all or none type of anger based on misconceptions of different situations and some form of annoyance towards person or thing.

Chronic Anger describes an ongoing form of anger that's typically based on some sort of resentment of life and of other people.

Vengeful Anger tends to be anger rooted in getting back at someone/something.

Petrified Anger tends to be a form of overwhelming anger that sees one shut down as a way of coping with the situation. Frustrated and giving up.

Constructive Anger is distinct from the other types of anger and can be a positive thing. It describes an anger that instead motivates positive reform in us.

Source: http://www.healthguidance.org

This is not a definitive list, but one that can help to self-assess the types of anger we may be feeling.

OVERCOMING ANGER

A few simple tips for gaining peace of mind and overcoming anger:

Think about on how much your life would be better without anger.

- You may try a deep breath and count slowly from one to ten.

Copyright © 2018 Michael E. Esser All rights reserved.
No part of this publication may be reproduced, distributed, or transmitted in any form or by any means

- Try drinking some water to calm the body.

- Thinking positive makes it easier to disregard remarks.

- Try to manifest at least some self-control and more common sense.

- Don't take everything too seriously. It is not worth it.

- Find reasons to laugh more often.

ASK YOURSELF, WHEN I GET UPSET, IS IT ABOUT <u>ME OR OTHERS</u>? (Circle one)

ASK YOURSELF, AM I AVOIDING SOMETHING IN MY LIFE THAT HAS ME FOCUSING ON OTHER PEOPLE? <u>YES OR NO</u> (Circle one)

ASK YOURSELF, DO I SOMETIMES MISS DRAMA SO MUCH I SEEK IT OUT?

HOW DO YOU STAY IN CONTROL WHEN YOU GET ANGRY?

REMEMBER THE THINGS YOU CAN CONTROL…

- YOU'RE WORDS, YOU'RE ACTIONS, AND YOU'RE IDEAS
- YOU'RE EFFORTS, YOU'RE MISTAKES AND YOU'RE BEHAVIOR

…AND WHAT YOU CAN'T

- OTHER PEOPLES WORDS

- OTHER PEOPLES ACTIONS

- OTHER PEOPLES IDEAS

- OTHER PEOPLES EFFORTS

- OTHER PEOPLES MISTAKES

- OTHER PEOPLES BEHAVIOR

Copyright © 2018 Michael E. Esser All rights reserved.
No part of this publication may be reproduced, distributed, or transmitted in any form or by any means

WEEKLY SELF-ASSESSMENT 15 – (COMPLETE/SHARE FOLLOWING)

Rate your SLEEP quality this week 1-10: _____ Rate your HEALTHY EATING this week 1-10: _____

Rate your EXERCISE/PHYSICAL ACTIVITY this week 1-10: _____

What's been your "BIGGEST STRUGGLE" over this past week?
On a scale of (1-to-10), rate this week's "struggle": (NOT BAD 1 - 2 - 3 - 4 - 5 - 6 - 7 - 8 - 9 - 10 WORST EVER)
What's the "BEST THING" you did or that happened to you this past week?
On a scale of (1-to-10), rate this week's "best thing": (NOT GREAT 1 - 2 - 3 - 4 - 5 - 6 - 7 - 8 - 9 - 10 BEST EVER)
What's the "MOST IMPORTANT THING YOU SHOULD BE DOING" this upcoming week?
On a scale of (1-to-10), rate how important it is to do "this thing": (NOT 1 - 2 - 3 - 4 - 5 - 6 - 7 - 8 - 9 – 10 VERY)
What would you rate your motivation this week? (NONE 1 - 2 - 3 - 4 - 5 - 6 - 7 - 8 - 9 – 10 TONS)
What would you rate your week overall? (ROUGH 1 - 2 - 3 - 4 - 5 - 6 - 7 - 8 - 9 – 10 AWESOME)
Was this past week better than the week before?   (YES) - (NO) - (SAME)
Finally, for every question you rated less than a 10, go back and ask yourself, "What made it less than a 10?" Then ask yourself, "What would it take for me to rate that question an 8+?" (These answers identify something we need to work on and what we need to do to fix it.)

Copyright © 2018 Michael E. Esser All rights reserved.

No part of this publication may be reproduced, distributed, or transmitted in any form or by any means

THOUGHT EXERCISES -SESSION 15: ANXIETY/COPING TECHNIQUES

Anxiety, or extreme uneasiness and worry, is a normal reaction to a stressful event or circumstances. However, in some cases, it becomes excessive and can cause sufferers to dread ordinary everyday situations. Needless to say, anxiety is another concern to our health that could have us trying to self-medicate or acting out in a way that leads us to commit another crime.

Anxiety can turn our world upside down because it is the body's perception that we are in danger. Your amygdala is a part of your brain that controls your systems responses to life and death/fight or flight responses. It is our minds security guard or warrior protector and sometimes, for no reason, it jumps into gear without any reason that our conscious mind understands.

Anxiety can present itself as difficulty breathing, headache, and stomach ache or even as sleep issues, sweating, or heart palpitations to name a few symptoms. For some, this can lead us to seek out some sort of relief or self-medication in the form of an unhealthy activity or substance use.

Knowing that anxiety is a common response, that more and more people are experiencing, can help us to not feel alone. Also knowing that there are things you can do to help relieve your anxiety is important too. But, if these symptoms become uncontrollable, seek professional help right away.

NAME IT, DRAW IT

Knowing that the amygdala is the part of the brain responsible for setting off the body's warning system gives us understanding. Giving that almond shaped part of the brain a "name" lets us address these feelings directly when they present themselves. Taking it a step further, by drawing a picture of that little "anxiety warrior" lets us visualize it. (Find a blank space and draw your anxiety warrior.)

Now when anxiety presents itself we can picture that responsible part of the brain and tell it by name that, "we've got this" and that, "it's okay to calm down."

HAPPY THOUGHT AND WALK AWAY

Another technique requires us to establish a "happy place" that we can visualize vividly. Then, when anxiety presents itself we stop, envision our happy place, and then physically walk or move away from the spot where the anxiety began.

Copyright © 2018 Michael E. Esser All rights reserved.
No part of this publication may be reproduced, distributed, or transmitted in any form or by any means

It's in this process that we can begin to fool our system into calling off the guard and calming down because we are flooding it with happy thoughts and physically moving away from the perceived danger.

SHARE YOUR EXPERIENCES WITH ANXIETY, IF ANY, WITH THE GROUP

COPING WITH STRESS

Once we get clean and/or have really begun to make real changes in our life, we are still going to have to deal with the problems that led to our drug abuse/crime. For example, were you trying to...

• Numb your emotions?

• Calm yourself down after a fight?

• Relax after a hard day?

• Forget about your struggles?

Even once you're sober, unresolved problems can and will resurface so we need to resolve these core issues if we're going to overcome our stress and the loneliness, frustration, anger, shame, and anxiety that accompany them. Finding actionable ways to work through these issues/feelings when they come up is a huge part of self-preservation and recovery.

RELIEVING STRESS WITHOUT DRUGS

Drug abuse often stems from misguided attempts to manage stress. We know it's easy to turn to alcohol or drugs to unwind and relax after a stressful event, or to cover up painful memories and emotions, but there are healthier ways to keep your stress level in check. The key is to become confident in your ability to de-stress because that'll let you face those kinds of strong feelings without them being as intimidating or overwhelming as they once were. Instead, try to engage your body and senses:

• Take a walk or do some body weight exercises to help find relief.

• Find a reason to smile. Play with your pet. Watch a comedy. Bake some cookies.

• Close your eyes and picture your happy place. Pamper yourself.

Source: https://www.helpguide.org

Copyright © 2018 Michael E. Esser All rights reserved.
No part of this publication may be reproduced, distributed, or transmitted in any form or by any means

WEEKLY SELF-ASSESSMENT 16 – (COMPLETE/SHARE FOLLOWING)

Rate your SLEEP quality this week 1-10: _____ Rate your HEALTHY EATING this week 1-10: _____

Rate your EXERCISE/PHYSICAL ACTIVITY this week 1-10: _____

What's been your "BIGGEST STRUGGLE" over this past week?
On a scale of (1-to-10), rate this week's "struggle": (NOT BAD 1 - 2 - 3 - 4 - 5 - 6 - 7 - 8 - 9 - 10 WORST EVER)
What's the "BEST THING" you did or that happened to you this past week?
On a scale of (1-to-10), rate this week's "best thing": (NOT GREAT 1 - 2 - 3 - 4 - 5 - 6 - 7 - 8 - 9 - 10 BEST EVER)
What's the "MOST IMPORTANT THING YOU SHOULD BE DOING" this upcoming week?
On a scale of (1-to-10), rate how important it is to do "this thing": (NOT 1 - 2 - 3 - 4 - 5 - 6 - 7 - 8 - 9 – 10 VERY)
What would you rate your motivation this week? (NONE 1 - 2 - 3 - 4 - 5 - 6 - 7 - 8 - 9 – 10 TONS)
What would you rate your week overall? (ROUGH 1 - 2 - 3 - 4 - 5 - 6 - 7 - 8 - 9 – 10 AWESOME)
Was this past week better than the week before?   (YES) - (NO) - (SAME)
Finally, for every question you rated less than a 10, go back and ask yourself, "What made it less than a 10?" Then ask yourself, "What would it take for me to rate that question an 8+?" (These answers identify something we need to work on and what we need to do to fix it.)

Copyright © 2018 Michael E. Esser All rights reserved.

No part of this publication may be reproduced, distributed, or transmitted in any form or by any means

THOUGHT EXERCISES - SESSION 16: CORE BELIEFS/PERCEPTIONS

CHALLENGE YOUR CORE BELIEFS

Understanding that we all see the world differently is important when it comes to addiction and criminal activity. Two people can go through the same experience and come out of it with completely different interpretations of what happened.

Our core beliefs are the engrained beliefs that we have that influence how we ultimately interpret our experiences. Think of them like the visor on your pilot helmet. Everyone has a different shade of visor on their helmet that has each of us seeing things differently. Ex:

Circumstances	Core belief	Result
You see a nice stranger sitting across from you in the coffee shop.	**Thought**: I'm not worthy	**Thought**: Why would they go for me? **Behavior**: You don't ask them out.
	Thought: I am worthy	**Thought**: We might have fun! **Behavior**: You ask them out!

Negative core beliefs can lead to harmful results that can have you seeking some sort of outside relief or self-medication.

Challenging those negative beliefs can only happen after we begin to identify what they are. Look at the following examples:

- *I'm not good enough / I'm ugly / I'm stupid / I'm boring / I'm a failure*

- *I'm worthless / I'm abnormal / I'm a bad person / I'm unlovable*

WHAT WAS THE FIRST CORE BELIEF TO JUMP OUT AT YOU?

NOW NAME TWO REASONS OR PIECES OF EVIDENCE THAT CONTRADICT THIS PARTICULAR NEGATIVE CORE BELIEF?

1. _____

2. _____

Copyright © 2018 Michael E. Esser All rights reserved.
No part of this publication may be reproduced, distributed, or transmitted in any form or by any means

YOU'RE LETTER OF ADVICE

For this exercise, write a letter giving advice to a friend or family member if they shared with you that they are going through everything you've gone through and in the middle of the same problem you are. How would you "coach" them? What if the person was your child? *SHARE YOUR LETTER*

Copyright © 2018 Michael E. Esser All rights reserved.
No part of this publication may be reproduced, distributed, or transmitted in any form or by any means

WEEKLY SELF-ASSESSMENT 17– (COMPLETE/SHARE FOLLOWING)

Rate your SLEEP quality this week 1-10: _____   Rate your HEALTHY EATING this week 1-10: _____

Rate your EXERCISE/PHYSICAL ACTIVITY this week 1-10: _____

What's been your "BIGGEST STRUGGLE" over this past week?
On a scale of (1-to-10), rate this week's "struggle": (NOT BAD 1 - 2 - 3 - 4 - 5 - 6 - 7 - 8 - 9 - 10 WORST EVER)
What's the "BEST THING" you did or that happened to you this past week?
On a scale of (1-to-10), rate this week's "best thing": (NOT GREAT 1 - 2 - 3 - 4 - 5 - 6 - 7 - 8 - 9 - 10 BEST EVER)
What's the "MOST IMPORTANT THING YOU SHOULD BE DOING" this upcoming week?
On a scale of (1-to-10), rate how important it is to do "this thing": (NOT 1 - 2 - 3 - 4 - 5 - 6 - 7 - 8 - 9 – 10 VERY)
What would you rate your motivation this week? (NONE 1 - 2 - 3 - 4 - 5 - 6 - 7 - 8 - 9 – 10 TONS)
What would you rate your week overall? (ROUGH 1 - 2 - 3 - 4 - 5 - 6 - 7 - 8 - 9 – 10 AWESOME)
Was this past week better than the week before?   (YES) - (NO) - (SAME)
Finally, for every question you rated less than a 10, go back and ask yourself, "What made it less than a 10?" Then ask yourself, "What would it take for me to rate that question an 8+?" (These answers identify something we need to work on and what we need to do to fix it.)

Copyright © 2018 Michael E. Esser All rights reserved.

No part of this publication may be reproduced, distributed, or transmitted in any form or by any means

THOUGHT EXERCISES -SESSION 17: 12 STEP INTROS TO AA

Alcoholics Anonymous is a non-profit, self-supporting, anonymous network of meetings and individuals that promote sobriety free of charge and welcome all. The concept is one that we've all heard of and some have participated or are actively involved.

Accompanying one of the biggest tools AA uses, "The Twelve Steps of Alcoholics Anonymous," are its use of meetings – scheduled around the clock – in which those seeking recovery can attend. These support groups are a key element identified by those with a lot of sober years under their belts. It provides a gathering place of like-minded individuals who are all seeking the same thing. It is a place to "connect" or "reconnect" with the world in a healthy way that is not only an outlet for the individual, but a place to learn from others.

Here we want to _simply introduce the concept of the twelve steps_.

THE TWELVE STEPS OF ALCOHOLICS ANONYMOUS

1. We admitted we were powerless over alcohol, that our lives had become unmanageable.

2. Came to believe that a Power greater than ourselves could restore us to sanity.

3. Made a decision to turn our will and our lives over to the care of God as we understood Him.

4. Made a searching and fearless moral inventory of ourselves.

5. Admitted to God, to ourselves, and to another human being the exact nature of our wrongs.

6. Were entirely ready to have God remove all these defects of character.

7. Humbly asked Him to remove our short-comings.

8. Made a list of all persons we had harmed, and became willing to make amends *to them all.

9. Made direct amends to such people wherever possible, except when to do so would injure them or others.

Copyright © 2018 Michael E. Esser All rights reserved.
No part of this publication may be reproduced, distributed, or transmitted in any form or by any means

10. Continued to take personal inventory and when we were wrong promptly admitted it.

11. Sought through prayer and meditation to improve our conscious contact with God as we understood Him, praying only for knowledge of His will for us and the power to carry that out.

12. Having had a spiritual awakening as the result of these steps, we tried to carry this message to alcoholics, and to practice these principles in all our affairs.

It is through these steps that thousands have come to a better understanding of themselves and their addictions. These steps provide a process that can help some gain the insight they need to overcome the adversity and obstacles in their lives and replace those things with a happier, healthier outlook on living a sober lifestyle.

BASIC INTERPRETATION OF 12 STEPS

There are several breakdowns that those in the program use to better understand or relate to the twelve steps. One of these translations might be:

1. Do you admit you have a problem?

2. Do you believe there's a scenario that you don't have a problem?

3. Are you, on your own, going to fix the problem?

4. Write down all the things that you've done or have ever done and don't lie, or leave anything out. (on separate private piece of paper)

5. Honestly tell someone trustworthy about your wrong doings.

6. Well, that's revealed a lot of patterns. Do you want to stop it?

7. Are you willing to live in a new way that's not all about you and your previous problems?

8. Prepare to apologize to everyone for everything affected by your problems.

9. Now apologize. Unless that would make things worse.

10. Watch out for problem thinking and behavior and be honest when it happens.

11. Stay connected to your new problem free/problem reduced perspective.

Copyright © 2018 Michael E. Esser All rights reserved.
No part of this publication may be reproduced, distributed, or transmitted in any form or by any means

12. Don't be a problem. Look at life less selfishly, be nice to everyone, and help people if you can.

THE SERENITY PRAYER

The Serenity Prayer is another common tool uses by those in AA. It is a prayer written by the American theologian Reinhold Niebuhr (1892–1971) and its best-known form is:

"GOD, GRANT ME THE SERENITY TO ACCEPT THE THINGS I CANNOT CHANGE,

COURAGE TO CHANGE THE THINGS I CAN,

AND WISDOM TO KNOW THE DIFFERENCE."

It is in this quote that we learn a few truths that can help on our journey.

DISCUSS HOW THE FOLLOWING PERTAIN TO THE SERENITY PRAYER

1. *Accepting something as it is, is not lazy.*

2. *Courage is the key to changing ourselves.*

3. *Adversity can be a good thing*

4. *Submitting requires bravery.*

5. *Joy and satisfaction are achievable both now and in the future.*

*DOES AA/NA SEEM LIKE SOMETHING YOU'D BE INTERESTED IN? (YES OR NO)

IF SO, VISIT *WWW.AA.ORG* OR *WWW.NA.ORG* FOR MORE INFORMATION, EVENTS, AND A LOCAL MEETING FINDER.

ALTERNATIVE FAITH BASED PROGRAMS MIGHT BE AVAILABLE IN YOUR AREA. AN EXAMPLE OF THIS WOULD BE SOMETHING LIKE CELEBRATE RECOVERY AT *WWW.CELEBRATERECOVERY.COM*

Copyright © 2018 Michael E. Esser All rights reserved.
No part of this publication may be reproduced, distributed, or transmitted in any form or by any means

WEEKLY SELF-ASSESSMENT 18 – (COMPLETE/SHARE FOLLOWING)

Rate your SLEEP quality this week 1-10: _____ Rate your HEALTHY EATING this week 1-10: _____

Rate your EXERCISE/PHYSICAL ACTIVITY this week 1-10: _____

What's been your "BIGGEST STRUGGLE" over this past week?
On a scale of (1-to-10), rate this week's "struggle": (NOT BAD 1 - 2 - 3 - 4 - 5 - 6 - 7 - 8 - 9 - 10 WORST EVER)
What's the "BEST THING" you did or that happened to you this past week?
On a scale of (1-to-10), rate this week's "best thing": (NOT GREAT 1 - 2 - 3 - 4 - 5 - 6 - 7 - 8 - 9 - 10 BEST EVER)
What's the "MOST IMPORTANT THING YOU SHOULD BE DOING" this upcoming week?
On a scale of (1-to-10), rate how important it is to do "this thing": (NOT 1 - 2 - 3 - 4 - 5 - 6 - 7 - 8 - 9 – 10 VERY)
What would you rate your motivation this week? (NONE 1 - 2 - 3 - 4 - 5 - 6 - 7 - 8 - 9 – 10 TONS)
What would you rate your week overall? (ROUGH 1 - 2 - 3 - 4 - 5 - 6 - 7 - 8 - 9 – 10 AWESOME)
Was this past week better than the week before?   (YES) - (NO) - (SAME)
**Finally, for every question you rated less than a 10, go back and ask yourself, "What made it less than a 10?" Then ask yourself, "What would it take for me to rate that question an 8+?" (These answers identify something we need to work on and what we need to do to fix it.)**

Copyright © 2018 Michael E. Esser All rights reserved.

No part of this publication may be reproduced, distributed, or transmitted in any form or by any means

THOUGHT EXERCISES -SESSION 18: REVIEW 9-17 + COPING SKILLS REVIEW

Going back and reviewing the past few sessions is something we'll do throughout this workbook. To do this, you will go back and review each session and answer the following questions or summary requests.

1. WHAT'S SOMETHING FROM SESSION 9 THAT HAS STUCK WITH YOU?

_____

(COMPLETE THE FOLLOWING SENTENCE IN THE SPACE PROVIDED)

"IN SESSION NINE WE LEARNED… _____

_____

_____."

2. WHAT'S SOMETHING FROM SESSION 10 THAT HAS STUCK WITH YOU?

_____

(COMPLETE THE FOLLOWING SENTENCE IN THE SPACE PROVIDED)

"IN SESSION TEN WE LEARNED… _____

_____

_____."

3. WHAT'S SOMETHING FROM SESSION 11 THAT HAS STUCK WITH YOU?

_____

"IN SESSION ELEVEN WE LEARNED… _____

_____

_____."

4. WHAT'S SOMETHING FROM SESSION 12 THAT HAS STUCK WITH YOU?

_____

"IN SESSION TWELVE WE LEARNED… _____

_____

_____."

Copyright © 2018 Michael E. Esser All rights reserved.
No part of this publication may be reproduced, distributed, or transmitted in any form or by any means

5. WHAT'S SOMETHING FROM SESSION 13 THAT HAS STUCK WITH YOU?

_____

(COMPLETE THE FOLLOWING SENTENCE IN THE SPACE PROVIDED)

"IN SESSION THIRTEEN WE LEARNED... _____

_____

_____."

6. WHAT'S SOMETHING FROM SESSION 14 THAT HAS STUCK WITH YOU?

_____

(COMPLETE THE FOLLOWING SENTENCE IN THE SPACE PROVIDED)

"IN SESSION FOURTEEN WE LEARNED... _____

_____

_____."

7. WHAT'S SOMETHING FROM SESSION 15 THAT HAS STUCK WITH YOU?

_____

"IN SESSION FIFTEEN WE LEARNED... _____

_____

_____."

8. WHAT'S SOMETHING FROM SESSION 16 THAT HAS STUCK WITH YOU?

_____

"IN SESSION SIXTEEN WE LEARNED... _____

_____

_____."

9. WHAT'S SOMETHING FROM SESSION 17 THAT HAS STUCK WITH YOU?

_____

"IN SESSION SEVENTEEN WE LEARNED... _____

_____

_____."

Copyright © 2018 Michael E. Esser All rights reserved.
No part of this publication may be reproduced, distributed, or transmitted in any form or by any means

COPING SKILLS:

Try to ground your thinking/feelings; focus on your breathing, pay attention to your senses, bake cookies for the smell, slowly eat them for the taste, walk on thick carpet or grass barefoot, exercise, listen to soft music. **Pro**: Helps you slow down and reduce anxiety

Release your emotions; let yourself feel your emotions, cry, scream, watch a funny video, turn up the music, go to a sauna, take a cold shower. **Pro**: relieves the pressure of anger and fear

Practice loving yourself more; get a massage, make your bed, take a bubble bath. **Pro**: You are worth it! Be your own best friend. Helps with guilt or shame.

END OF LEVEL I AND II – COMPLETE FINALS

Copyright © 2018 Michael E. Esser All rights reserved.
No part of this publication may be reproduced, distributed, or transmitted in any form or by any means

BUILDING A MAINTENANCE PLAN (SELF-PACED EXERCISE)

PART ONE: BUILDING A MAINTENANCE / STRENGTHS

IDENTIFY YOUR STRENGTHS (CIRCLE YOUR TOP TEN)

Assertive	Inspiring	Dedicated
Enthusiastic	Adventurous	Flexible
Spontaneous	Lively	Happy
Honest	Persuasive	Logical
Trustworthy	Serious	Open
Respectful	Idealistic	Accurate
Tolerant	Warm	Independent
Observant	Humorous	Intelligent
Optimistic	Friendly	Tactful
Caring	Determined	Creative
Generous	Patient	Honest
Practical	Orderly	Straightforward
Considerate	Disciplined	Appreciative
Self-assured	Ambitious	Versatile

- ***Now cut that list of ten down to five***

- ***Now cut that list of five down to three***

- ***Now cut that list of three down to two, and then one***

Know that you possess all ten of these strengths. Just by cutting them down you discover what strengths you value most. This exercise helps you to identify and own your strengths in ways that'll continue to help you solve life's problems.

Congratulations! We'll use these strengths to complete our maintenance plan.

Copyright © 2018 Michael E. Esser All rights reserved.
No part of this publication may be reproduced, distributed, or transmitted in any form or by any means

REVIEW: OLD BEHAVIORS VS. NEW LIFE

OLD LIFE: WHAT IS RELAPSE TO YOU?

NEW LIFE: WHAT IS RECOVERY TO YOU?

When presented with everyday life's pressures, what are some of the negative things you might *start* doing?

What about positive things you might *stop* doing? How do you handle social pressures?

What are your urges and cravings triggers?

What has helped you cope with them in the past?

Describe a good attitude versus a bad attitude.

What emotions do you find uncomfortable? Why?

How have you stayed on track when you experience these painful emotions?

How do you resolve outside conflict and stay sober?

Copyright © 2018 Michael E. Esser All rights reserved.
No part of this publication may be reproduced, distributed, or transmitted in any form or by any means

BUILDING A MAINTENANCE PLAN (SELF-PACED EXERCISE)

PART TWO: MAINTENANCE PLAN BUILDING / SKILLS

ANSWER THE FOLLOWING:

Willingness or the state of being prepared to do something; readiness.

How you benefit from being willing?

Honesty is honor, integrity, and correctness of character or action. Honesty implies a refusal to lie, steal, or deceive in any way.

How would you consider yourself honest?

Gratitude or emotion expressing appreciation for what one has, as opposed to being driven by what one wants.

How can you use gratitude to make positive changes?

Responsible or the state of being the person who caused something to happen. A duty or task that you are required or expected to do.

How will responsibility help you achieve your goals?

Being open-minded or having or showing a mind receptive to new ideas or arguments.

How will being open-minded help you?

Thoughtful or displaying kindness and concern for others.

How can you work towards being a more thoughtful person in life?

Copyright © 2018 Michael E. Esser All rights reserved.
No part of this publication may be reproduced, distributed, or transmitted in any form or by any means

Fair means a lack of bias, judgment, or prejudice.

How can being fair help you make positive changes?

Being humble or the quality or condition of being humble; modest opinion or estimate of one's own importance, rank, etc.

How can being humble help your behavior when make positive changes?

STRATEGIES FOR CHANGE REVIEW

- Get the facts - investigate

- Explore what's in your best interests – what's right, not what you want

- Examine your thinking – challenge your beliefs

- Lead by example – be a role model

- Consider public support – outside yourself/groups

- Make a commitment – set a goal

- Use substitutes – replace bad with good

- Seek supports – seek a role model/trusted individual

- Manage your environment – make your environment match your goals

- Use rewards – reward yourself for positive steps

CONTROLLED THINKING REVIEW

In this exercise we look at our thinking…

AUTOMATIC APPROACH (NOT THINKING IT THROUGH REVIEW):

There's an event > we react automatically > we don't feel good about results

CONTROLLED APPROACH (THINK IT THROUGH REVIEW)

Copyright © 2018 Michael E. Esser All rights reserved.
No part of this publication may be reproduced, distributed, or transmitted in any form or by any means

<u>Check our perceptions</u> - Am I right? How would others think about this event? > <u>Challenge beliefs</u> - Am I being rational? > <u>Examine choices</u> - Does thinking this way make me feel good or the way I want? Will my thoughts help or hurt me?

STRATEGIES FOR SELF-CONTROL REVIEW

- Coach yourself – "stay in control" "don't rush into anything"

- Stop and think – time out

- Seek compromise – look at both sides and seek the win-win

- Be prepared – for any foreseeable triggers

- Keep options open – don't put yourself in the corner

- Don't get sucked in – know other people might try to get you to act out

- Take a deep breath – it helps

- Do a mental rewind – remember past events that didn't turn out so well

- Seek help and support – look for honest feedback

COMMUNICATION REVIEW

- Always start with active listening and pay attention to your body language. Then, be sure to always talk as clearly as possible.

SUPPORT NETWORK REVIEW

- Mentors/role models: those that show by example your desired behaviors

- Healthy peers: new / existing healthy individuals

- Supportive family members: positive, supportive people in your family

- Skilled help: counselors, probation officer, pastor, etc. Trained individuals

OUT OF ALL THIS REVIEWED INFORMATION, WHAT STANDS OUT AS RELATING THE MOST TO YOU AND YOUR LIFE?

Copyright © 2018 Michael E. Esser All rights reserved.
No part of this publication may be reproduced, distributed, or transmitted in any form or by any means

BUILDING A MAINTENANCE PLAN (SELF-PACED EXERCISE)

MAINTENANCE PLAN BUILDING/BUILD IT

EVERYDAY LIFE PRESSURES

Pick one of the strengths you identified and describe how it can help you manage your everyday life's pressures and worries.

STRENGTH:

HOW IT CAN HELP:

Pick a skill and describe how you'll use it to keep balance in your life.

(Being Positive /Be adaptable/Controlled thinking/Self-Control/Have a Conversation/Turn to Support Network)

SKILL:

HOW YOU'LL USE IT:

SOCIAL PRESSURE

Pick one of your strengths you identified and describe how it can help you to respond to the pressure of social burdens.

STRENGTH:

HOW IT CAN HELP:

Pick a skill and describe how you'll use it to respond to social pressure.

(Being Positive /Be adaptable/Controlled thinking/Self-Control/Have a Conversation/Turn to Support Network)

SKILL:

HOW YOU'LL USE IT:

Copyright © 2018 Michael E. Esser All rights reserved.

No part of this publication may be reproduced, distributed, or transmitted in any form or by any means

URGES AND CRAVINGS

Pick one of your strengths you identified and describe how it can help you to manage urges and cravings.

STRENGTH:

HOW IT CAN HELP:

Pick a skill and describe how you'll use it to manage urges and cravings.

(Being Positive /Be adaptable/Controlled thinking/Self-Control/Have a Conversation/Turn to Support Network)

SKILL:

HOW YOU'LL USE IT:

BAD ATTITUDE

Pick one of your strengths you identified and describe how it can help you to overcome bad attitudes.

STRENGTH:

HOW IT CAN HELP:

Pick a skill and describe how you'll use it to overcome negative attitudes.

(Being Positive /Be adaptable/Controlled thinking/Self-Control/Have a Conversation/Turn to Support Network)

SKILL:

HOW YOU'LL USE IT:

Copyright © 2018 Michael E. Esser All rights reserved.
No part of this publication may be reproduced, distributed, or transmitted in any form or by any means

PAINFUL EMOTIONS

Pick one of your strengths you identified and describe how it can help you deal with painful emotional.

STRENGTH:

HOW IT CAN HELP:

Pick a skill and describe how you'll use it to deal with uncomfortable emotions.

(Being Positive /Be adaptable/Controlled thinking/Self-Control/Have a Conversation/Turn to Support Network)

SKILL:

HOW YOU'LL USE IT:

OUTSIDE CONFLICT

Pick one of your strengths you identified and describe how it can help you to respond to resolve outside conflict.

STRENGTH:

HOW IT CAN HELP:

Pick a skill and describe how you'll use it to resolve conflict with others.

(Being Positive /Be adaptable/Controlled thinking/Self-Control/Have a Conversation/Turn to Support Network)

SKILL:

HOW YOU'LL USE IT:

Copyright © 2018 Michael E. Esser All rights reserved.
No part of this publication may be reproduced, distributed, or transmitted in any form or by any means

LIFE SKILLS LESSON: EMPLOYMENT

WHY WORK?

Working is good for our health and welfare. It adds to our contentment in life, it helps us to shape our confidence and our self-esteem, all while rewarding us financially. It is because of these benefits that it is important to work and return to work as soon as possible after being sick or injured.

BENEFITS OF WORK:

- Keeps us busy, challenges us and gives us the means to develop

- Gives us a sense of pride, identity and individual accomplishment

- Enables us to socialize, build our support networks

- Provides us with the financial means to support ourselves and hobbies

HEALTH BENEFITS OF WORKING

People who work tend to enjoy healthier, more content lives than those who aren't working. Even our physical and mental health is generally improved through the regular, consistent schedule working requires.

Because of these health benefits, we are all encouraged to find employment and remain employed, if our health permits it.

HEALTH BENEFITS OF RETURNING TO WORK

Being out of work has a destructive impact on our health and welfare. People who are unemployed:

- Have higher rates of physical and mental health problems

- Take more medication and use more medical services

- Have a shorter life expectancy

Returning to work after a period of being without a job results in significant physical and mental health developments, even so much as to help in reversing the negative health effects of the time spent being unemployment.

Copyright © 2018 Michael E. Esser All rights reserved.
No part of this publication may be reproduced, distributed, or transmitted in any form or by any means

GETTING A JOB – BREAKING DOWN THE PROCESS

FINDING JOB OPPORTUNITIES

- Search online

- Use social media

- Utilize your state job bank

- Start networking

- Spread the word that you are job hunting

- Attend a job fair

PREPARING YOURSELF

- Match your resume to the job description

- Create an elevator speech, or a 30-sec. pitch of why you're a good hire

APPLYING FOR JOBS

- Carefully read the job description

- Apply online or in-person – based on employer's preference

- The interview

  - Dress professionally

  - Make eye contact and speak confidently

  - Arriving early is arriving on time!

FOLLOW UP, FOLLOW UP, FOLLOW UP

- This is the *real* key that, so many job seekers don't consider or do. If you want the job, show up enough times that they remember your tenacity.

WHAT TIPS HAVE YOU FOUND WORK WHEN IT COMES TO EMPLOYMENT? WHAT KIND OF JOB DO YOU REALLY WANT? WHAT KIND OF JOB ARE YOU WILLING TO DO WHILE YOU WORK TOWARDS THAT GOAL JOB?

Copyright © 2018 Michael E. Esser All rights reserved.
No part of this publication may be reproduced, distributed, or transmitted in any form or by any means

LIFE SKILLS LESSON: MONEY MANAGEMENT

PROTECTING YOUR MONEY

Once we have a job and are earning money, we need to protect it. This means having an account either at a bank or through some sort of a prepaid card - after all, everything from bills to shopping and dining are going to want us to be able to pay digitally – and health insurance to protect our health/ability to earn.

Protection goes beyond simply "securing" your finances in a way that can't easily be stolen or lost – and if there are any misappropriations of funds or fraud your company will assist you in getting that money back. We also need to be able to protect our money from ourselves. That's right. We need to be able to distinguish between our, "needs, wants, and goals."

- **NEEDS**: rent, power bill, food, etc.

- **WANTS**: new video game, fancy coffee, going out to eat

- **GOALS**: savings account, bills paid on time,

We must respect ourselves and the effort it took to earn our money. When we do this, we pay attention to everything we spend and that means keeping receipts, knowing your exact balances in each account – if multiple, and calendaring your payment due dates at least a month in advance.

BASIC MONEY MANAGEMENT TIPS

Save for an emergency. Having money to fall back on and building our own little emergency nest egg will give us piece of mind and security to live happier and healthier lives. (Think 1-6 months' worth of bills.)

Pay attention to any credit card, debit card, and loan offers. It is crucial that we learn how to read and understand the terms and conditions of basic credit agreements. Annual fees, late fees, and other unknowns can cause you to sign up for something you can't afford or will cause you more harm than good.

Build a positive credit history. Having no credit history these days can be just as bad as having poor credit history. We need to understand how to build credit, how to be responsible with it, and why being responsible with it is a key to long-

Copyright © 2018 Michael E. Esser All rights reserved.
No part of this publication may be reproduced, distributed, or transmitted in any form or by any means

term stability and security. There are free websites and services that can help you to better manage your credit like Credit Karma and Credit Wise.

Never taking what we have for granted is key. We never know when something can change, and we want to be prepared so that this new, healthier life we are building remains just that. Money stresses are one of the biggest problems we all face at some time or another. Being prepared and smart means we'll have enough in place to stand up to these situations.

Source: http://www.moneymanagement.org

BASIC BUDGET

1. Track your money for one month.

2. List all income for the month and make savings plan.

3. Compare expenses to income.

4. Determine what changes you can make to achieve your goals.

5. Review budget every so often, adjust as necessary.

INCOME FROM ALL SOURCES: _____

SAVINGS: _____

EXPENSES:

- Rent: _____
- Insurance: _____
- Power/Gas/Water: _____
- Internet: _____
- Phone(s): _____
- Food: _____
- Entertainment: _____

- Fees/Fines: _____
- Misc: _____
- Misc: _____

PUTTING IT ALL TOGETHER:

>INCOME: _____

\- SAVINGS: _____

\- EXPENSES: _____

= SURPLUS: _____

HOW DID YOUR BUDGET TURN OUT? WAS IT WHAT YOU EXPECTED? DID YOU FIND MONEY THAT YOU PREVIOUSLY DIDN'T THINK WAS THERE? WHAT ARE YOU SPENDING THIS MISSING MONEY ON?

Copyright © 2018 Michael E. Esser All rights reserved.
No part of this publication may be reproduced, distributed, or transmitted in any form or by any means

POST-TEST – TRUE OR FALSE – FINAL PART ONE*

__ In the U.S., nearly one-third of all traffic deaths involve alcohol

__ Drivers with .08 BAC+ killed in a crash were 4.5x more likely to have prior DUI

__ On average only 1% of those that drink, and drive are arrested each year

__ BAC stands for blood alcohol concentration

__ At any level BAC, younger people are not at a greater risk than older people

__ Alternatives to driving drunk/high are calling cab, take bus, designated driver

__ Relapse happens in stages; emotional, mental, and physical

__ Automatic thinking can get us in trouble if we have unhealthy beliefs

__ Addiction can be the result of some sort of personal disconnection in one's life

__ You are not responsible for your behavior or making any needed changes

__ Reconnecting with ourselves, our purpose, and others helps addiction

__ Being completely honest with oneself is essential for recovery

__ The body can only process 1 drink per hour so only time will sober one up

__ Empathy is putting yourself in someone else's place to better understand them

__ Personal boundaries are just about having 3 feet of space around you

__ Cravings are thoughts we have, and urges are actions we take

__ Having a healthy support network like mentors and healthy peers is important

__ Isolating yourself from others is an unhealthy way of coping with grief

__ Anxiety is a result of your amygdala perceiving that you are in danger

__ It's not important to identify your personal strengths when bettering yourself

__ Getting enough sleep each night is crucial to your mental and physical health

__ In addition; diet, exercise, knowledge, and love are all pillars of healthy living

Copyright © 2018 Michael E. Esser All rights reserved.
No part of this publication may be reproduced, distributed, or transmitted in any form or by any means

UPDATE OF YOUR RELAPSE PREVENTION PLAN – FINAL PART TWO**

Will you include any of the following in your relapse prevention plan?
Self-Help Programs like A.A., N.A., Celebrate Recovery, etc. *Yes or No*
A Proper Diet *Yes or No*
An Exercise Program Important *Yes or No*
A Spiritual Development Program *Yes or No*
Morning and Evening Inventories *Yes or No*

As a way of premeditating your response in the future, answer the following:
What direct action can I take when I am feeling lonely?

What direct action can I take when I am feeling nervous?

What direct action can I take when I am feeling frustrated or angry?

What direct action can I take when I'm not getting along with friends and family?

What direct action can I take when recovery begins to feel boring/unimportant?

Make a list of high risk people and places you will avoid:
High risk people I will avoid:
High risk places I will avoid:

Who is someone who can give you support in times of need? (Name/Number)

What are the signs and symptoms that indicate I am heading toward relapse?

What are the consequences if I relapse?
To Self:
To Family:
To Society:

What are the benefits if I remain in recovery?
To Self:
To Family:
To Society:

Copyright © 2018 Michael E. Esser All rights reserved.
No part of this publication may be reproduced, distributed, or transmitted in any form or by any means

EXIT INTERVIEW WORKSHEET – FINAL PART THREE***

At this point, let's be sure you are:

- Focusing on your capability rather than the problem.

- Focusing on finding your unique solution.

- Focusing your energy on being optimistic.

- Remembering your past successes, so they can help build confidence now.

- Aware that you are the expert about "you".

- Setting goals to put you on the best path toward change.

- Aware that you are responsible for the changes in your life.

PART ONE:

1. *What was the charge or problem that brought you to this program?*

2. *How has this charge or problem affected your life?*

3. *How do you feel about this?*

4. *What do you think you need to do about this moving forward?*

5. *What's different this time?*

6. *If you don't maintain this change, then what?*

7. *If you do maintain this change, then what happens?*

8. *What do you want to do?*

9. *On a scale of 1 to 10, how committed are you to this change?*

10. *Why did you choose that number?*

PART TWO:

1. *Whose responsibility is it to solve this problem?*

2. *If the options are: Treatment/No longer have these things in your life, Prison, or Death – What's your choice?*

Copyright © 2018 Michael E. Esser All rights reserved.
No part of this publication may be reproduced, distributed, or transmitted in any form or by any means

3. *Do you believe your situation has happened to others before?*

4. *Do you believe you can do it? I DO, NOW PROVE THIS TO YOURSELF.*

PART THREE (CLEARING IT ALL UP):

1. *Do you understand the problem?*

2. *What is your goal?*

3. *What have you tried in the past that didn't work?*

4. *What could you do or have done different?*

5. *What will you do the next time you face this problem?*

PART FOUR (PUTTING IT ALL TOGETHER):

Based on your answers, write a 50-word summary as a letter to yourself.

_____

_____

_____

_____

_____

_____

_____

_____

(PRE-POST TEST ANSWER KEY: T-T-T-T-F-T-T-T-T-F-T-T-T-T-F-T-T-T-T-F-T-T)

Copyright © 2018 Michael E. Esser All rights reserved.

No part of this publication may be reproduced, distributed, or transmitted in any form or by any means

SELF-PRESERVATION/PROGRAM COMPLETION INFORMATION

PARTICIPANTS FULL NAME: _____

ADDRESS: _____

CITY/STATE/ZIP: _____

PHONE: _____

EMAIL: _____

COURT NAME: _____

DOCKET NUMBER: _____

ADDRESS: _____

CITY/STATE/ZIP: _____

PHONE: _____

EMAIL: _____

FACILITATOR NAME: _____

AGENCY: _____

ADDRESS: _____

CITY/STATE/ZIP: _____

COMPLETION DATE: _____

FACILITATOR SIGNATURE: _____

MISC. INFO/NOTE: _____

Copyright © 2018 Michael E. Esser All rights reserved.
No part of this publication may be reproduced, distributed, or transmitted in any form or by any means

Made in the USA
Monee, IL
04 August 2021

74864783R10061